D0482623

JOYFUL

WISDOM

ALSO BY YONGEY MINGYUR RINPOCHE

WITH ERIC SWANSON

THE JOY OF LIVING

Library of Congress Cataloging-in-Publication Data

Yongey Mingyur, Rinpoche, 1976–
Joyful wisdom / Yongey Mingyur Rinpoche and Eric Swanson.
    p. cm.
1. Spiritual life—Buddhism. 2. Buddhism—Doctrines. I. Swanson, Eric. II. Title.
BQ4302.Y66 2009
294.3'444—dc22
2008050424

ISBN 978-0-307-40779-5

Printed in the United States of America

Design by Jo Anne Metsch

10 9 8 7 6 5 4 3 2 1

First Edition

JOYFUL
WISDOM

Embracing Change and Finding Freedom

YONGEY MINGYUR RINPOCHE

WITH ERIC SWANSON

HARMONY BOOKS

NEW YORK

Contents

CONTENTS

JOYFUL
WISDOM

INTRODUCTION

In the middle of difficulty lies opportunity.
—ALBERT EINSTEIN

ON A RECENT teaching tour of North America, I was told by a student that an influential philosopher of the twentieth century had called the era in which we live the "age of anxiety."

"Why?" I asked him.

He explained to me that, according to this philosopher, two bloody world wars had left a kind of emotional scar in people's minds. Never before had so many people been killed in warfare—and worse, the high death toll was a direct result of industrial and scientific advances that were supposed to have made human life more civilized and comfortable.

Since those terrible wars, he went on to say, nearly every advance we've made in terms of material comfort and convenience has had a shadow side. The same technological breakthroughs that have given us cell phones, supermarket scanners, ATMs, and personal computers are the basis for creating weapons that can wipe out entire populations and perhaps destroy the planet we call home. E-mail, the Internet, and other computer technologies that were supposed to make our lives easier often overwhelm us with too much information and too many possibilities, all supposedly urgent, demanding our attention.

The news we hear, he continued—online, in magazines and newspapers, or on TV—is overwhelmingly unpleasant: full of crises, violent images, and predictions of worse to come. I asked him why these reports focus so much on violence, crime, and terrorism rather than on the good deeds that people have done and the successes that people have accomplished.

"Bad news sells," he replied.

I didn't understand that phrase, and asked him what he meant.

"Disasters get people's attention," he explained. "People are drawn to bad news because it confirms our worst fears that life is unpredictable and scary. We're always on the lookout for the next terrible thing so we can perhaps prepare against it—whether it's a stock market crash, a suicide bomb, a tidal wave, or an earthquake. 'Aha,' we think, 'I was *right* to be scared . . . now let me think about what I can do to protect myself.'"

As I listened to him, I realized that the emotional climate he was describing wasn't at all unique to the modern age. From the twenty-five-hundred-year-old perspective of Buddhism, every chapter in human history could be described as an "age of anxiety." The anxiety we feel now has been part of the human condition for centuries. In general, we respond to this basic unease and the disturbing emotions that arise from it in two distinct ways. We try to escape or we succumb. Either route often ends up creating more complications and problems in our lives.

Buddhism offers a third option. We can look directly at the disturbing emotions and other problems we experience in our lives as stepping-stones to freedom. Instead of rejecting them or surrendering to them, we can befriend them, working through them to reach an enduring, authentic experience of our inherent wisdom, confidence, clarity, and joy.

"How do I apply this approach?" many people ask. "How do I take my life on the path?" This book is, in many ways, a response to their questions: a practical guide to applying the insights and practices of Buddhism to the challenges of everyday life.

It's also meant for people who may not be experiencing any problems or difficulties at the moment; people whose lives are proceeding quite happily and contentedly. For these fortunate individuals it serves as an examination of the basic conditions of human life from a Buddhist perspective that may prove useful, if only as a means of discovering and cultivating a potential of which they might not even be aware.

In some ways, it would be easy just to organize the ideas and methods discussed in the following pages as a simple instruction manual—the kind of pamphlet you get when you buy a cell phone, for instance. "Step One: Check to make sure that the package includes all of the following . . ." "Step Two: Remove the battery cover on the back of the phone." "Step Three: Insert the battery." But I was trained in a very traditional fashion, and it was instilled in me from a young age that a basic understanding of the principles—what we might call the view—was essential in order to derive any real benefit from practice. We have to understand our basic situation in order to work with it. Otherwise, our practice goes nowhere; we're just flailing around blindly without any sense of direction or purpose.

For this reason, it seemed to me that the best approach would be to organize the material into three parts, following the pattern of classical Buddhist texts. Part One explores our basic situation:

the nature and causes of the various forms of unease that condi-tion our lives and their potential to guide us toward a profound recognition of our own nature. Part Two offers a step-by-step guide through three basic meditation practices aimed at settling our minds, opening our hearts, and cultivating wisdom. Part Three is devoted to applying the understanding gained in Part One and the methods described in Part Two to common emotional, physical, and personal problems.

While my own early struggles may contribute in some small way to the topics explored in the following pages, a far greater share of insight has come from my teachers and friends. I owe a special debt of gratitude, however, to the people I've met over the past twelve years of teaching around the world, who have spoken so candidly about their own lives. The stories they've told me have broadened my understanding of the complexities of emotional life and deep-ened my appreciation of the tools I learned as a Buddhist.

PART ONE

PRINCIPLES

Our life is shaped by the mind;

we become what we think.

—*The Dhammapada,*
translated by Eknath Easwaran

1

LIGHT IN THE TUNNEL

The sole purpose of human existence is to kindle a light in the darkness of mere being.

—Carl Jung, *Memories, Dreams, Reflections*, translated by Richard Winston and Clara Winston

SEVERAL YEARS AGO I found myself strapped inside an *f*MRI, a type of brain scanner that, to me, looked like a round, white coffin. I lay on a flat examination table that slid like a tongue inside the hollow cylinder which, I was told, held the scanning equipment. My arms, legs, and head were restrained so that it was nearly impossible to move, and a bite guard was inserted into my mouth to keep my jaws from moving. All the preparation—being strapped onto the table and so forth—was fairly interesting, since the technicians very courteously explained what they were doing and why. Even the sensation of being inserted into the machine was somewhat soothing, though I could see how someone with a very active imagination might feel as though he or she were being swallowed.

Inside the machine, however, it rapidly grew quite warm. Strapped in as I was, I couldn't wipe away any stray beads of sweat that crawled down my face. Scratching an itch was out of the question—and it's pretty amazing how itchy the body can get when there's not the slightest opportunity to scratch. The machine itself made a loud whirring noise like a siren.

Given these conditions, I suspect that spending an hour or so inside an *f*MRI scanner isn't something many people would choose to do. I'd volunteered, though, along with several other monks. Altogether, fifteen of us had agreed to undergo this uncomfortable experience as part of a neuroscientific study led by Professors Antoine Lutz and Richard Davidson at the Waisman Laboratory for Brain Imaging and Behavior in Madison, Wisconsin. The aim of the study was to examine the effects of long-term meditation practice on the brain. "Long-term" in this case meant somewhere between 10,000 and 50,000 hours of cumulative practice. For the younger volunteers, the hours had taken place over the course of perhaps fifteen years, while some of the older practitioners had been meditating for upwards of forty years.

As I understand it, an *f*MRI scanner is a bit different from a standard MRI, which employs powerful magnets and radio waves to produce—with the help of computers—a detailed still image of internal organs and body structures. While using the same magnet and radio wave technology, *f*MRI scanners provide a moment-by-moment record of changes in the brain's activity or function. The difference between the results of an MRI scan and the results of an *f*MRI scan is similar to the difference between a photograph and a video. Using *f*MRI technology, neuroscientists can track changes in various areas of the brain as subjects are asked to perform certain tasks—for example, listening to sounds, watching videos, or performing some sort of mental activity. Once the signals from the scanner are processed by a computer, the end result is a bit like a movie of the brain at work.

The tasks we were asked to perform involved alternating between certain meditation practices and just allowing our minds to rest in an ordinary or neutral state: three minutes of meditation followed by three minutes of resting. During the meditation periods we were treated to a number of sounds that could, by most standards, be described as quite unpleasant—for example, a woman screaming and a baby crying. One of the goals of the experiment was to determine what effect these disagreeable sounds had on the brains of experienced meditators. Would they interrupt the flow of concentrated attention? Would areas of the brain associated with irritation or anger become active? Perhaps there wouldn't be any effect at all.

In fact, the research team found that when these disturbing sounds were introduced, activity in areas of the brain associated with maternal love, empathy, and other positive mental states actually increased.[1] Unpleasantness had triggered a deep state of calmness, clarity, and compassion.

This finding captures in a nutshell one of the main benefits of Buddhist meditation practice: the opportunity to use difficult conditions—and the disturbing emotions that usually accompany them—to unlock the power and potential of the human mind.

Many people never discover this transformative capacity or the breadth of inner freedom it allows. Simply coping with the internal and external challenges that present themselves on a daily

[1]See Lutz, A., Brefczynski-Lewis, J., Johnstone, T., Davidson, R.J. (2008) "Regulation of the Neural Circuitry of Emotion by Compassion Meditation: Effects of Meditative Expertise." *PLoS ONE* 3(3): e1897.

basis leaves little time for reflection—for taking what might be called a "mental step back" to evaluate our habitual responses to day-to-day events and consider that perhaps there may be other options. Over time, a deadening sense of inevitability sets in: *This is the way I am, this is the way life works, there's nothing I can do to change it.* In most cases, people aren't even aware of this way of seeing themselves and the world around them. This basic attitude of hopelessness sits like a layer of sludge on the bottom of a river, present but unseen.

Basic hopelessness affects people regardless of their circumstances. In Nepal, where I grew up, material comforts were few and far between. We had no electricity, no telephones, no heating or air-conditioning systems, and no running water. Every day someone would have to walk down a long hill to the river and collect water in a jug, carry it back uphill, empty the jug into a big cistern, and then trudge back down to fill the jug again. It took ten trips back and forth to collect enough water for just one day. Many people didn't have enough food to feed their families. Even though Asians are traditionally shy when it comes to discussing their feelings, anxiety and despair were evident in their faces and in the way they carried themselves as they went about the daily struggle to survive.

When I made my first teaching trip to the West in 1998, I naively assumed that with all the modern conveniences available to them, people would be much more confident and content with their lives. Instead, I discovered that there was just as much suffering as I saw at home, although it took different forms and sprang from different sources. This struck me as a very curious phenomenon. "Why is this?" I'd ask my hosts. "Everything's so great here. You have nice homes, nice cars, and good jobs. Why is there so much unhappiness?" I can't say for sure whether Westerners are simply more open to talking about their problems or whether the people I asked were just being polite. But before long, I received more answers than I'd bargained for.

In short order, I learned that traffic jams, crowded streets, work deadlines, paying bills, and long lines at the bank, the post office, airports, and grocery stores were common causes of tension, irritation, anxiety, and anger. Relationship problems at home or at work were frequent causes of emotional upset. Many people's lives were so crammed with activity that finally coming to the end of a long day was enough to make them wish that the world and everybody in it would just *go away* for a while. And once people did manage to get through the day, put their feet up, and start to relax, the telephone would ring or the neighbor's dog would start barking—and instantly whatever sense of contentment they may have settled into would be shattered.

Listening to these explanations, I gradually came to realize that the time and effort people spend on accumulating and maintaining material or "outer wealth" affords very little opportunity to cultivate "inner wealth"—qualities such as compassion, patience, generosity, and equanimity. This imbalance leaves people particularly vulnerable when facing serious issues like divorce, severe illness, and chronic physical or emotional pain. As I've traveled around the world over the past decade teaching courses in meditation and Buddhist philosophy, I've met people who are completely at a loss when it comes to dealing with the challenges life presents them. Some, having lost their jobs, are consumed by a fear of poverty, of losing their homes, and of never being able to get back on their feet. Others struggle with addiction or the burden of dealing with children or other family members suffering from severe emotional or behavioral problems. An astonishing number of people are crippled by depression, self-hatred, and agonizing low self-esteem.

Many of these people have already tried a number of approaches to break through debilitating emotional patterns or find ways to cope with stressful situations. They're attracted to Buddhism because they've read or heard somewhere that it offers a novel method of overcoming pain and attaining a measure of peace and well-being. It often comes as a shock that the teachings and practices laid out by the Buddha twenty-five hundred years ago do not in any way involve conquering problems or getting rid of the sense of loneliness, discomfort, or fear that haunts our daily lives. On the contrary, the Buddha taught that we can find our freedom only through embracing the conditions that trouble us.

I can understand the dismay some people feel as this message sinks in. My own childhood and early adolescence were colored so deeply by anxiety and fear that all I could think of was escape.

RUNNING IN PLACE

> *To the extent that one allows desire (or any other emotion) to express itself, one correspondingly finds out how much there is that wants to be expressed.*
>
> —Kalu Rinpoche, *Gently Whispered*, compiled, edited, and annotated by Elizabeth Selandia

As an extremely sensitive child, I was at the mercy of my emotions. My moods swung dramatically in response to external situations. If someone smiled at me or said something nice, I'd be happy for days. The slightest problem—if I failed a test, for example, or if someone scolded me—I wanted to disappear. I was especially nervous around strangers: I'd start to shake, my throat would close up, and I'd get dizzy.

The unpleasant situations far outnumbered the pleasant ones, and for most of my early life the only relief I could find was by running away into the hills surrounding my home and sitting by myself in one of the many caves there. These caves were very special places where generations of Buddhist practitioners had sat for long periods in meditative retreats. I could almost feel their presence and the sense of mental calmness they'd achieved. I'd imitate the posture I'd seen my father—Tulku Urgyen Rinpoche, a great meditation master—and his students adopt, and I'd pretend to meditate. I'd had no formal training as yet, but just sitting there, feeling the presence of these older masters, a sense of stillness would creep over me. Time seemed to stop. Then, of course, I'd come down from the caves and my grandmother would scold me for disappearing. Whatever calmness I'd begun to feel would instantly evaporate.

Things got a little better around the age of nine, when I started training formally with my father. But—and this is a little embarrassing to admit for someone who travels around the world teaching meditation—while I liked the *idea* of meditation and the promise it represented, I really didn't like the practice. I'd itch; my back would hurt; my legs would go numb. So many thoughts buzzed through my mind that I found it impossible to focus. I'd be distracted by wondering, "What would happen if there was an earthquake, or a storm?" I was especially afraid of the storms that swept through the region, which were quite dramatic, full of lightning and booming thunder. I was, truth be told, the very model of the sincere practitioner who never practices.

A good meditation teacher—and my father ·was one of the best—will usually ask his or her students about their meditation experiences. This is one of the ways a master gauges a student's development. It's very hard to hide the truth from a teacher skilled in reading the signs of progress, and even harder when that teacher is your own father. So, even though I felt I was disappointing him, I really didn't have any choice except to tell him the truth.

As it turned out, being honest was the best choice I could have made. Experienced teachers have, themselves, usually passed through most of the difficult stages of practice. It's very rare for someone to achieve perfect stability the first time he or she sits down to meditate. Even such rare individuals have learned from their own teachers and from the texts written by past masters about the various types of problems people face. And, of course, someone who has taught hundreds of students over many years will have undoubtedly heard just about every possible complaint, frustration, and misunderstanding that will arise over the course of training. The depth and breadth of knowledge such a teacher accumulates makes it easy to determine the precise remedy for a particular problem and to have an intuitive understanding of precisely how to present it.

I'm forever grateful for the kind way my father responded to my confession that I was so hopelessly caught up by distractions that I couldn't follow even the simplest meditation instructions, like focusing on a visual object. First, he told me not to worry; distractions were normal, he said, especially in the beginning. When people first start to practice meditation all sorts of things pop up in their minds, like twigs carried along by a rushing river. The "twigs" might be physical sensations, emotions, memories, plans, even thoughts like "I can't meditate." So it was only natural to be carried away by these things, to get caught up, for instance, in wondering, *Why can't I meditate? What's wrong with me? Everyone else in the room seems to be able to follow the instructions, why is it so hard for me?* Then he explained that whatever was passing through my mind at any given moment was *exactly* the right thing to focus on, because that was where my attention was anyway.

It's the act of paying attention, my father explained, that gradually slows the rushing river in a way that would allow me to experience a little bit of space between what I was looking at and the simple awareness of looking. With practice, that space would grow longer and longer. Gradually, I'd stop identifying with the thoughts, emotions, and sensations I was experiencing and begin to identify with the pure awareness of experience.

I can't say that my life was immediately transformed by these instructions, but I found great comfort in them. I didn't have to run away from distractions or let distractions run away with me. I could, so to speak, "run in place," using whatever came up—thoughts, feelings, sensations—as opportunities to become acquainted with my mind.

MAKING FRIENDS

We must be willing to be completely ordinary people, which means accepting ourselves as we are.

—Chögyam Trungpa Rinpoche, *The Myth of Freedom*

The Tibetan word for meditation is *gom*, which, roughly translated, means "to become familiar with." Going by this definition, meditation in the Buddhist tradition may perhaps best be understood as a process of getting to know your mind. It's actually very simple, like meeting someone at a party. Introductions are made—"Hello, my name is . . ." Then you try to find a common point of interest: "Why are you here? Who invited you?" All the while, though, you're looking at this other person, thinking about the color of his or her hair, the shape of the face, whether he or she is tall or short, and so on.

Meditation, getting to know your mind, is like that in the beginning: an introduction to a stranger. That may sound a little odd at first, since most of us tend to feel that we already know what's going on in our minds. Typically, however, we're so accustomed to the flow of thoughts, emotions, and sensations that we rarely stop to look at them individually—to greet each with the openness we would offer a stranger. More often than not, our experiences pass through our awareness more or less as mental, emotional, and sensory aggregates—a collection of details that appear as a singular, independent whole.

To use a very simple example, suppose you're driving along on the way to work and suddenly encounter a traffic jam. Although your mind registers the event as "traffic jam," actually, a lot of things are occurring. You decrease the pressure of your foot on the gas pedal and increase pressure on the brake. You observe the cars ahead, behind, and on either side of you slow down and stop. The nerves in your hands register the sensation of holding on to the steering wheel while the nerves in your back and legs are registering contact with the seat. Perhaps the noise of car horns penetrates your window. At the same time, you may be thinking, "Oh, no, I'm going to be late for my morning meeting," and in a flash you start running through a kind of mental "script" associated with being late. Your boss might be angry; you might miss important information; or maybe you were supposed to give a presentation to your coworkers. Then your heart starts beating a little faster and maybe you start to sweat. You might find yourself getting angry with the drivers up ahead and start tapping the car horn in frustration. Yet even though so many processes—physical, mental, and emotional—occur simultaneously, they all appear to the conscious mind as a single, cohesive experience.

According to the cognitive scientists I've spoken with, this tendency to roll many different strands of experience into a single package represents the normal operation of the human mind. Our brains are constantly processing multiple streams of information through our sense organs, evaluating them against past experience, and preparing the body to respond in certain ways—for example, releasing adrenaline into the bloodstream to heighten our awareness in potentially dangerous situations. At the same time, areas of the brain associated with memory and planning start spinning out thoughts: "How far ahead is traffic congested? Should I dig out my cell phone and call someone? Maybe I should wait it out for a little bit. I think there's an exit not too far from here. I could get off there and take a different route. Hey, that car over there is trying to cut ahead on the side of the road." Further, because the areas associated with reason, memory, and planning are closely linked with the areas that generate emotional responses, whatever thoughts arise are typically colored by some sort of feeling—which, in the case of a traffic jam, or my own response to the thunderstorms, is usually unpleasant.

For the most part, these processes occur spontaneously, beyond the range of ordinary consciousness. Less than one percent of the information our brains receive through the senses actually reaches our awareness. The brain competes for limited resources of attention, sifting out what it judges unnecessary and homing in on what appears to be important. In general, this is quite a useful arrangement. If we were acutely conscious of every stage of the process involved in an activity as simple as walking from one room to another, we'd be so quickly overcome by the details of lifting one foot and setting down another, small changes in the air around us, the color of the walls, levels of sound, and so on, that we probably wouldn't get very far. And if we did manage to get to the next room, we might not remember what we wanted to do when we arrived!

The disadvantage of this arrangement, however, lies in the fact that we end up mistaking a very small fraction of our moment-by-moment experience for the whole. This can cause problems when we're faced with an uncomfortable situation or a strong emotion. Our attention fixes on the most intense aspect of whatever we're experiencing—physical pain, the fear of being late, the embarrassment of failing an exam, the grief of losing a friend. In general, our minds spin in one of two directions when faced with such situations: We try to escape or we become overwhelmed. Our experience appears to us as either an enemy or, by completely taking over our thoughts and manipulating our reactions, a "boss." Even if we do manage to temporarily escape whatever is bothering us—turning on the TV, reading a book, or surfing the Internet—the problem just goes underground for a little while, secretly gaining more power because now it has become mixed with the fear of facing it again later on.

My father's advice to me, when I told him of the trouble I was having practicing meditation, offered a middle way between these two extremes. Instead of trying to block distractions or give in to them, I could welcome them as friends: "Hello, fear! Hello, itch!

How are you? Why don't you stick around awhile so we can get to know each other?"

This practice of gently welcoming thoughts, emotions, and sensations is commonly referred to as *mindfulness*—a rough translation of the Tibetan term *drenpa*, to become conscious. What we're becoming conscious of are all the subtle processes of mind and body that ordinarily escape our notice because we're focused on the "big picture," the dominant aspect of experience that hijacks our attention, overwhelming us or provoking an urge to escape. Adopting a mindful approach gradually breaks down the big picture into smaller, more manageable pieces, which flash in and out of awareness with amazing rapidity.

It's a bit astonishing, in fact, to discover how shy the mind becomes when you offer to make friends with it. Thoughts and feelings that seemed so powerful and solid vanish almost as soon as they appear, like puffs of smoke blown away by a strong wind. Like many people who begin to practice mindfulness, I found it quite difficult to observe even a tenth of what was passing through my mind. Gradually, though, the rush of impressions began very naturally to slow on its own; and as it did, I noticed several things.

First, I began to see that the sense of solidity and permanence I'd attached to disturbing emotions or distracting sensations was actually an illusion. A split-second twinge of fear was replaced by the beginning of an itch, which lasted only an instant before the sight of a bird outside the window caught my attention; then maybe someone would cough, or a question would pop up: "I wonder what we're having for lunch?" A second later, the fear would come back, the itch would get stronger, or the person sitting in front of me in my father's meditation room would shift position.

Watching these impressions come and go became almost like a game, and as the game progressed, I began to feel calmer and more confident. Without consciously intending it, I found myself becoming less scared of my thoughts and feelings, less troubled by distractions. Instead of a dark, controlling stranger, my mind was evolving into, if not precisely yet a friend, at least an interesting companion.

Of course, I could still get carried away by thoughts and day-dreams or shifting between states of restlessness and dullness. Again, my father advised me not to worry too much about such occurrences. Sooner or later, I'd remember to return to the simple task of observing whatever was happening in the present moment. The important point was not to judge myself for these lapses of attention. This proved to be an important lesson, because I often *did* judge myself for drifting off. But here again, the instruction to simply observe my mind produced a startling realization. Most of what troubled me consisted of judgments *about* my experience. "This is a good thought. This is a bad one. Oh, I like this feeling. Oh, no, I hate this one." My fear of fear was, in many cases, more intense than fear on its own. I felt for a while as if there were two separate rooms in my mind: one filled with thoughts, feelings, and sensations that I was gradually beginning to recognize, and another, secret back room occupied by chattering ghosts.

In time, I realized that the rooms weren't really separate. The chatter was going on alongside everything else I was thinking and feeling, though so faintly that I hadn't recognized it. By applying the same process of gently observing the running commentary in my mind, I began to see that these thoughts and feelings were ephemeral. As they came and went, the power of their hidden judgments began to fade.

During the few years I trained exclusively with my father, the extreme swings of mood that had haunted me in my early childhood diminished somewhat. I wasn't so easily swayed by praise or terrified by embarrassment or failure. I even found it a bit easier to talk to the many visitors who frequently came to my father for instruction.

Soon, though, my situation would change and I would face a challenge that required me to apply the lessons I'd learned on a much deeper level than I'd ever imagined.

OF ANTIDOTES AND BODYGUARDS

In Tibet there is an incredibly toxic root called tsenduk; *you don't have to eat much of it before you die. At the same time, this plant can also be used as medicine.*

—Tulku Urgyen Rinpoche, *As It Is, Volume I,*
translated by Erik Pema Kunsang

When I was eleven years old, I was sent from my father's hermitage in Nepal to Sherab Ling monastery in India—a journey of more than three thousand miles—to begin a rigorous course of study in Buddhist philosophy and practice. It was my first trip away from home and family, and my first experience on an airplane. Boarding the flight from Kathmandu to Delhi in the company of an older monk who served as my escort, I was seized by terror. What would happen if the plane suddenly lost power or was stuck by lightning? Images of the plane plunging from the sky and smashing to the ground filled my head, and I gripped the armrests of my seat so hard that my palms hurt. Blood rushed to my face as the plane took off and I sat rigid in my seat, sweating.

Seeing my discomfort, a man sitting beside me told me, with the confidence of a seasoned traveler, that there was really nothing to worry about; the plane was quite safe, he said, smiling, and since the flight was short—only one hour—we'd be landing before I knew it. His kind words restored my nerves a little bit, and I sat for a while trying to practice watching my mind as I'd been taught. Then, suddenly we hit some turbulence. The plane shook and the man almost jumped out of his seat, yelping in panic. For the rest of the flight, I sat immobilized, imagining the worst. Forget about watching my mind. I was sure I was going to die.

Fortunately, the thirteen-hour drive from Delhi to Sherab Ling was much less eventful. In fact, as we approached the mountains in which the monastery is located, the view became expansive and the drive quite pleasurable.

Unbeknownst to me, however, a reception at the monastery had been planned for my arrival. Many of the resident monks had lined up on the hill overlooking the road, waiting to greet me with eight-foot-long ceremonial horns and large, heavy drums. Since there was no telephone communication in that area at the time, the assembly had been waiting quite a while, and when they finally saw a car approaching, they started blowing the horns and beating the drums. But when the car stopped, a young Indian woman stepped out—obviously not me—and the grand reception came to an abrupt and embarrassing halt as the bewildered woman made her way through the gates.

Some time passed before my car was spotted along the road and the monks began blowing long blasts on their horns and beating their drums. But as my car approached the main entrance, confusion again disrupted the proceedings. I am, even as an adult, not a very tall person. As a child, I was so short that my head couldn't be seen past the high, old-fashioned dashboard. From where the musicians stood, there didn't seem to be anyone sitting in the front passenger seat. Unwilling to make another mistake, they lowered their horns and drum sticks and the music came to a stumbling halt.

When the passenger door was opened and I stepped out, I was greeted by such a loud, enthusiastic fanfare that I could feel the vibrations in my bones. I'm not sure which was more alarming: the noise of the instruments or the sight of all those strangers lined up to welcome me. All the terror I'd felt on the airplane came rushing back, and I made a wrong turn, walking off in the wrong direction. If it weren't for the monk who'd accompanied me, I'm not sure I would have made it through the entrance gate at all.

It was not a particularly auspicious beginning to my stay at Sherab Ling. In spite of the fact that the monastery itself—nestled between the Himalayas to the north and east and rolling flatlands to the south and west—was very beautiful, I was for the most part miserably unhappy. My old sensitivity and anxiety came back with overwhelming force, defeating my best efforts to welcome them as my father had taught me. I had trouble sleeping and little things could set off a chain reaction of disturbing thoughts. I remember quite vividly, for example, waking up one morning and discovering a tiny crack in the window of my bedroom. For weeks afterwards I was terrified that the housekeeper would blame me for breaking the window and for the trouble it would cause to replace the glass.

Group practice sessions were especially painful. There were about eighty monks in residence at the time, and they all seemed quite friendly with one another, strolling between classes and practice sessions in groups, laughing and joking. I was a stranger among them. Except for our robes, I didn't feel we had anything in common. When we sat down in the main hall for group rituals, they all knew the words and the gestures much better than I, and I wondered whether they were watching me, waiting for me to make a mistake. Most of these sessions were accompanied by horns, drums, and cymbals—a sometimes deafening roar of music that made my heart pound and my head spin. I wanted so badly to run out of the hall, but with all those others watching, there was no escape.

The only moments of real comfort I experienced came during my private lessons with my tutors Drupon Lama Tsultrim, who taught me language, ritual, and philosophy, and Saljay Rinpoche, who instructed me in meditation practices. I felt an especially close connection with Saljay Rinpoche, a very wise lama with a squarish head and gray hair and, despite being in his eighties, a face almost unwrinkled by age. In my mind's eye, I can still see him with his prayer wheel in one hand and his *mala*—a set of beads used to count repetitions of *mantras*, special combinations of ancient syllables that form a sort of prayer or which, more generally, can be used as a support for meditation—in the other. His kindness and patience were so great that I came to view him almost as a second father, to whom I could bring problems both great and small.

His responses invariably wound up as profound lessons. For instance, one morning while washing my hair, a little bit of water got trapped in my ear. I tried everything to get rid of it: wiping the inside of my ear with a towel, shaking my head, twisting little bits of tissue paper inside my ear. Nothing helped. When I told Saljay Rinpoche about it, he advised me to pour more water in my ear, then tip my head to let it all drain out. To my surprise, it worked!

This, Rinpoche explained, was an example of the principle, taught long ago by the Buddha, of using the problem as the antidote. Timidly, I asked if the same approach could be used to deal with thoughts and feelings. He looked at me quizzically, and soon I found myself pouring out the whole story of how anxious I'd been most of my life; the fear that sometimes attacked with such violence I could hardly breathe; how I'd tried to watch my mind in a friendly, nonjudgmental way as my father had taught me; my small successes back in Nepal, where everything was familiar; and how all the old problems had resurfaced even more forcefully in this new, strange environment.

He listened until I ran out of words and then replied with the following story.

"Tibet," he said, "is full of long and lonely roads, especially in the mountains, where there aren't many towns or villages. Traveling is always dangerous, because there are almost always bandits hiding in caves or behind rocks along the sides of the road, waiting to jump out and attack even the most watchful travelers. But what can people do? To get from one place to another, they have to take those roads. They can travel in groups, of course, and if the groups are big enough, maybe the bandits won't attack. But that doesn't always work, because the bandits will usually see an opportunity to steal more from a larger group. Sometimes people try to protect themselves by hiring bodyguards. But that doesn't work very well, either."

"Why not?" I asked.

He laughed. "The bandits are always more fierce and they have better weapons. Besides, if fighting breaks out, there's more of a chance that people will get hurt."

His eyes closed, his head drooped, and I thought maybe he'd fallen asleep. But before I could think of any way to wake him, he opened his eyes and continued.

"The clever travelers, when attacked by bandits, make a deal with them. 'Why don't we hire you to be our bodyguards? We can pay you something now and more when we reach the end of our journey. That way, there won't be any fighting, no one will get hurt, and you'll get more from us than you would by simply robbing us on the trail. Less danger for you, because no one will come hunting you in the mountains, and less danger for us, because you're stronger and have better weapons than any bodyguards we could hire. And if you keep us safe along the road, we can recommend you to other people and soon you'll be earning more than you could ever hope to gain by robbing people. You could have a nice home, a place to raise a family. You wouldn't have to hide in caves, freezing in the winter and boiling in the summer. Everybody benefits.'"

He paused, waiting to see if I understood the lesson. My expression must have given away that I hadn't, so he continued.

"Your mind is the long and lonely road, and the all the problems you described are the bandits. Knowing that they're there, you're afraid to travel. Or you use mindfulness like a hired bodyguard, mixing it with hope and fear, thinking, 'If I watch my thoughts, they'll disappear.' Either way, your problems have the upper hand. They'll always seem bigger and stronger than you are.

"A third choice is to be like a clever traveler and invite your problems to come with you. When you're afraid, don't try to fight the fear or run from it. Make a deal with it. 'Hey, fear, stick around. Be my bodyguard. Show me how big and strong you are.' If you do that often enough, eventually fear becomes just another part of your experience, something that comes and goes. You become comfortable with it, maybe even come to rely on it as an opportunity to appreciate the power of your mind. Your mind must be very powerful to produce such big problems, yes?"

I nodded. It seemed logical.

"When you no longer resist a powerful emotion like fear," he continued, "you're free to channel that energy in a more constructive direction. When you hire your problems as bodyguards, they show you how powerful your mind is. Their very fierceness makes you aware of how strong you are."

BREAKTHROUGH

The best way out is always through.
—Robert Frost,
"A Servant to Servants"

I'd never thought of the emotional storms I suffered as evidence of the power of my own mind. Or rather, I'd heard teachings to that effect, especially from my father, who would frequently point out that disturbing emotions are actually expressions of the mind—in the same way that intense heat, for example, is a product or expression of the sun. But like most people when they first start the practice of examining their minds, I was more concerned with getting rid of the thoughts and feelings that upset me than with actually looking directly at their source. As Saljay Rinpoche pointed out, my efforts in practicing mindfulness were bound up in hope and fear: the hope that by watching my thoughts the unpleasant ones would eventually fade away, and the fear that when they resurfaced, I'd be stuck with them forever.

Looking back, I can see that my early attempts weren't all that different from the strategies that people typically use when faced with challenging situations or powerful emotions. I was trying to think my way through anxiety and panic, laboring under the assumption that there was something desperately wrong and if I could just get rid of the problems, everything would be okay; my life would be blissful, serene, and trouble-free. The essence of Saljay Rinpoche's lesson was to consider the possibility that the thoughts and feelings that kept me awake at night and made my heart pound like a trapped bird during the day were actually signs of something *right*: as if my mind were reaching out to say, "Look at me! Look what I can do!"

Some people can grasp such a radical alternative right away. My father, I've heard, was such a person. As soon as he heard the teaching on the nature of the mind, he intuitively grasped that all experience is a product of the mind's unlimited capability—"the magical display of awareness" as it's often described in Buddhist texts. Unfortunately, I am not that quick. My progress was more of the "two steps forward, one step back" variety that I heard about from students later on when I started teaching. It took a crisis for me to finally face my fears head on and recognize their source.

That crisis occurred during the first year of the three-year retreat program at Sherab Ling—a period of intensive training in the essential and advanced forms of Tibetan Buddhist meditation, which can only be passed on orally by a teacher who has received the oral transmissions and mastered them sufficiently to pass them on to a new generation of students. This tradition of passing the teachings down orally is a kind of protective seal, preserving the teachings in their original form in an unbroken lineage stretching back more than a thousand years. They're offered in a sequestered setting—you're literally locked away from the outside world as a means of minimizing distractions, in order to focus more directly and intensely on the inner landscape of the mind.

Because I was only thirteen at the time, there was some doubt that I'd be allowed to enter the retreat. In general, this opportunity is offered to older students who have had more opportunity to achieve a solid foundation in basic practices like mindfulness training. But Saljay Rinpoche was going to be the principal teacher, and I was so eager to study under him that I pressed my father to intervene on my behalf. Ultimately my request was granted. Joyously, I took the retreat vows along with the other participants and settled into my cloistered room.

It didn't take long for me to regret my decision.

Dealing with troubling thoughts and emotions in an open setting is hard enough for most people—but at least there are opportunities for distraction, especially nowadays with cable TV, the Internet, e-mail, and cell phones so readily available. Even a walk in the woods can offer some "breathing room" for the mind. But in a three-year retreat setting, such opportunities are limited. There are group teachings and practices—which I still hated—and long periods of solitary practice, during which there's nothing to do except watch your mind. After a while, you can begin to feel trapped: small annoyances start to feel huge and more intense thoughts and emotions become powerful, threatening giants. Saljay Rinpoche compared the experience to planning a visit to a park or wilderness. You pack up food and other provisions for a day of quiet relaxation in a beautiful setting, and shortly after you settle in, government officials arrive with orders from the king or minister saying that you can't leave the park under any conditions. Enforcers surround you in four directions, frowning and refusing to let you move from your spot. Even if you try to appease them by smiling, they remain standing there, stone-faced—resisting any spontaneous urges to return your smile. Your whole experience changes in that instant. Instead of being able to enjoy your surroundings, all you can think of is figuring out how to escape. Unfortunately, there is no escape.

I started avoiding group practices, hiding in my room. But in some ways that was worse, because I couldn't hide from my mind. I trembled; I sweated; I tried to sleep. In the end, I had little choice but to apply the teachings I'd received—starting off gently, according to the first lessons I'd learned from my father, just watching my thoughts and emotions as they came and went, observing their transitory nature. After the first day, I found myself able to welcome them, to become, in a way, fascinated by their variety and intensity—an experience that one of my students describes as looking through a kaleidoscope and noticing how the patterns change. By the third day, I began to understand, not intellectually, but rather in a direct, experiential way, what Saljay Rinpoche meant about bodyguards: how thoughts and emotions that seemed overwhelming were actually expressions of the infinitely vast and endlessly inventive power of my own mind.

I emerged from my room the next day and began to participate once again in group practices with much greater confidence and clarity than I'd ever dreamed possible.

I can't say that I never experienced any mental or emotional "bumps" over the remainder of the retreat. Even now, almost twenty years later, I'm still subject to the range of ordinary human experiences. I'm hardly what anyone would call enlightened. I get tired, as other people do. Sometimes I feel frustrated or angry or bored. I look forward to the occasional breaks in my teaching schedule. I get cold quite easily.

However, having learned a bit about working with my mind, I've found that my relationship to these experiences has shifted. Instead of being completely overwhelmed by them, I've begun to welcome the lessons they offer. Whatever challenges I face nowadays have become opportunities to cultivate a broader, deeper level of awareness—a transformation that, with practice, occurs more and more spontaneously, similar to the way a swimmer automatically directs more energy to his muscles when hitting a turbulent patch of water and emerges stronger and more confident after the ordeal. I find the same thing happening when I get angry or tired or bored. Rather than fixate on the mental or emotional turbulence itself or look for its cause, I attempt to see it as it is: a wave of the mind, an expression of its uninhibited power.

So overall, though my life is far from perfect, I'm contented with it. And in a peculiar way, I'm grateful for the troubling emotions I experienced as a child. The obstacles we face in life can provide powerful incentives for change.

A student I met with during a recent trip to Canada put it this way:

"Anxiety had always been a problem for me, especially at work. I felt I wasn't doing a good enough job or working fast enough; that other people were talking behind my back and that because I wasn't as quick or competent as others, I'd lose my job. And if I lost my job, how would I support myself and my family? How would I put food on the table? These thoughts would go on and on until I actually felt myself *experiencing* the horror of living on the street, holding a cup and begging for coins.

"The only way I could calm myself down was to look for a 'light at the end of the tunnel'—desperately hoping that conditions would change. That I'd get a new job that was less demanding. Or that the pressure would decrease. Maybe I'd get a new manager. Or maybe the people whispering behind my back would get fired.

"Then I started looking at the anxiety itself, and I began to see that the problem wasn't the job but the thoughts I was having *about* my job. Looking for that 'light at the end of the tunnel' was nothing more than the flip side of fear—a hope that a change in circumstances would rescue me from the panic. Gradually, I began to realize that hope and fear were also nothing more than ideas floating through my mind. They really had nothing to do with the job itself.

"In that moment, it hit me that the light I was looking for *was* the tunnel and that the tunnel I felt trapped in *was* the light. The only difference between them was my perspective—the way I chose to look at my situation.

"That shift in perspective has made all the difference. When I feel anxious or afraid, I can look at that those impulses and see that I have a choice. I can surrender to them or I can observe them. And if I choose to observe them, I learn more about myself and the power I have to make decisions about how I respond to the events in my life."

This man's story reminded me of my experience in the *f*MRI—a tunnel of sorts, in which the challenges of heat, noise, screams, and crying might easily have been disconcerting, but which became, instead, opportunities to discover a more vivid sense of peace, clarity, and compassion. My early training and the experiences that followed have shown me that what may at first appear as darkness is, in essence, nothing more substantial than a shadow cast by the mind's true light.

2

THE PROBLEM IS THE SOLUTION

And the end of all our exploring
Will be to arrive where we started
And know the place for the first time.
            —T.S. ELIOT, "Little Gidding"

NOT LONG AGO I visited a wax museum in Paris, where I saw a very lifelike statue of the Dalai Lama. I examined it carefully from all angles, since His Holiness is a person I know fairly well. As I stood to the side looking at the figure, a young man and woman walked up. The woman knelt down between His Holiness and me while her companion aimed his camera for a picture. Not wanting to get in the way, I started to step aside—at which point the woman screamed and the man with the camera dropped his jaw almost to the ground. Because the light in the museum was rather dim, they'd thought I was part of the display: a wax figure of a happy little monk standing beside the Dalai Lama.

Once the couple recovered from the shock of seeing what appeared to be a wax statue suddenly springing to life, we all had a nice laugh together and parted company on a very pleasant note. But as I continued on through the museum, it occurred to me how that brief encounter had exposed, on a small scale, a larger and fundamentally tragic aspect of the human condition. The young couple had approached the wax museum display with such a clear, strong set of expectations, never considering the possibility that the actual situation might be otherwise than they'd assumed. In the same way, most people, encumbered by all sorts of preconceptions and beliefs, remain ignorant of the fundamental facts of human life—what my teachers called "the basic situation."

To understand what that situation is, we need to look at the very first teachings the Buddha gave after he attained what is often referred to as *enlightenment*—a term that can sound a bit grand, beyond the capacity of most people.

Actually, enlightenment is quite simple. Think of it in terms of habitually walking through a dark room, bumping into tables, chairs, and other bits of furniture. One day, by luck or accident, we brush against a switch or button that turns on a light. Suddenly we see all the room, all the furniture in it, the walls, and the rugs, and think, "Look at all this stuff here! No wonder I kept bumping into things!" And as we look at all this stuff, perhaps with a sense of wonder at seeing it for the first time, we realize that the light switch was always there. We just didn't know it, or maybe we just didn't think about the possibility that the room could be anything but dark.

That's one way to describe enlightenment: turning on the light in a room we've spent most of our lives navigating in the dark.

Perhaps the most remarkable achievement of the Buddha is his delivery of the message that we've become so used to walking in the dark that we've forgotten how to turn on the light.

THE FOUR NOBLE TRUTHS

We may now have a life endowed with the freedoms and advantages which are so difficult to find, but it will not last for long.

—Patrul Rinpoche, *Words of My Perfect Teacher*,
translated by the Padmakara Translation Group

The Buddha was a somewhat unusual teacher, in that he didn't begin his career by making any grand metaphysical pronouncements. He focused instead on what would be immediately practical to the greatest number of people. To fully grasp the clarity and simplicity of his approach, it may be helpful to cut through the mythology that has grown up around his life and attempt to see the man behind the myth.

Legend holds that Siddārtha Gautama—the name he was given at birth—was a prince, the son of a tribal chieftain in northern India. At the celebration honoring his birth, a Brahmin seer predicted that he would grow up to be either a powerful king or a great holy man. Fearing that his eldest son would forsake his role as a tribal leader, the Buddha's father built for him a network of pleasure palaces that would shield him from exposure to any of the troubling aspects of life that might awaken any latent spiritual inclinations. At the age of sixteen, he was urged to marry and produce an heir.

But fate intervened. At the age of twenty-nine, determined to visit his subjects, he ventured outside his palaces, and in the process encountered people who were poor, aged, ill, or dying.

Disturbed by this confrontation with the realities of suffering from which he'd been protected for so many years, he slipped away and traveled south, where he met several ascetics who encouraged him to free his mind from worldly concerns through practicing strict methods of renunciation and self-mortification. Only in doing so, they taught, could he free himself from the mental and emotional habits that entrap most people in an endless round of inner and outer conflict.

But after six years of practicing extreme austerity, he grew frustrated. Withdrawal from the world didn't provide the answers he sought. So, although he suffered the ridicule of his former companions, he gave up the practice of completely withdrawing from the world. He took a nice, long bath in the nearby Nairajana River and accepted food from a woman who was passing by. He then crossed the river to the place now called Bodhgaya, propped himself under a ficus tree, and began to examine his mind. He was determined to discover a way out of the all too human dilemma of perpetuating problems through chasing after things that provide, at best, fleeting experiences of happiness, safety, and security.

When he emerged from his examination, he realized that true freedom lay not in withdrawal from life, but in a deeper and more conscious engagement in all its processes. His first thought was that "No one will believe this." Whether motivated, according to the legends, by pleas from the gods or by an overwhelming compassion for others, he eventually left Bodhgaya and traveled west toward the ancient city of Varanasi, where, in an open space that has come to be known as the Deer Park, he encountered his former ascetic companions. Though at first inclined to dismiss him because he'd given up the way of extreme austerity, they couldn't help but notice that he radiated a poise and contentment that surpassed anything they'd achieved. They sat down to listen to what he had to say. His message was quite compelling and so logically sound that the men who listened became his first followers, or disciples.

The principles he outlined in the Deer Park, commonly referred to as "The Four Noble Truths," consist of a simple, direct analysis of the challenges and possibilities of the human condition. This analysis represents the first of what is often referred to in historical terms as "The Three Turnings of the Wheel of Dharma": a progressive set of insights into the nature of experience, which the Buddha delivered at different stages during the forty-five years he spent traveling throughout ancient India.

Each turning, building on the principles expressed in the previous one, offers deeper and more penetrating insights into the nature of experience. The Four Noble Truths form the core of all Buddhist paths and traditions. In fact, the Buddha felt they were so important that he gave them many times, to many different audiences. Along with his later teachings, they have been handed down to us in a collection of writings known as the *sutras*—conversations considered to be the actual exchanges between the Buddha and his students.

For several centuries after the Buddha's death, these teachings were transmitted orally—a not uncommon practice during a period in which many people were illiterate. Eventually, some three or four hundred years after the Buddha's passing, these oral transmissions were committed to writing in Pali, a literary language believed to be closely related to the dialect spoken in central India during the Buddha's lifetime. Later they were transcribed into Sanskrit, the high literary grammar of ancient India. As Buddhism spread across Asia and later to the West, they have been translated into many different languages.

Even in translations of the *sutras,* it's plain to see that the Buddha didn't present the Four Noble Truths as a set of concrete practices and beliefs. Instead, he offered the Four Noble Truths as a practical guide for individuals to recognize, in terms of their own lives, their basic situation, the causes of the situation, the possibility that the situation might be transformed, and the means of transformation. With supreme skill, he structured this initial teaching in terms of the classical Indian four-point method of medical practice: diagnosing the problem, identifying the underlying causes, determining the prognosis, and prescribing a course of treatment. In a way, the Four Noble Truths can be seen as a pragmatic, step-by-step approach to healing what we might nowadays call a "dysfunctional" perspective that binds us to a reality shaped by expectations and preconceptions and blinds us to the inherently unlimited power of the mind.

IDENTIFYING THE PROBLEM

> *As humans, we also suffer from not getting what we want and not keeping what we have.*
>
> —Kalu Rinpoche, *Luminous Mind: The Way of the Buddha,*
> translated by Maria Montenegro

The first of the Four Noble Truths is known as the Truth of Suffering. The *sutras* related to these teachings have been translated in many ways over the centuries. Depending on the translation you read, you might find this basic principle of experience stated as "There is suffering," or even more simply, "Suffering is."

At first glance, the first of the Four Noble Truths might seem quite depressing. Upon hearing or reading it many people are apt to dismiss Buddhism as unduly pessimistic. "Oh, those Buddhists are always complaining that life is miserable! The only way to be happy is to renounce the world and go off to a mountain somewhere and meditate all day. How boring! I'm not miserable. My life is wonderful!"

It's important, first of all, to note that Buddhist teachings don't argue that in order to find true freedom people have to give up their homes, their jobs, their cars, or any other material possessions. As his own life story shows, the Buddha himself had tried a life of extreme austerity without finding the peace he sought.

Moreover, there's no denying that, for some people, circumstances can come together for a while in such a way that life seems like it couldn't get any better. I've met a lot of people who appear quite satisfied with their lives. If I ask them how they're doing, they'll answer, "Fine," or "Just great!" Until, of course, they get sick, lose their jobs, or their children reach adolescence and overnight are transformed from affectionate bundles of joy into moody, restless strangers who want nothing to do with their parents. Then, if I ask how things are going, the reply changes a little: "I'm fine, except . . ." or "Everything's great, but . . ."

This is, perhaps, the essential message of the First Noble Truth: Life has a way of interrupting, presenting even the most contented among us with momentous surprises. Such surprises—along with subtler, less noticeable experiences like the aches and pains that come with age, the frustration of waiting in line at the grocery store, or simply running late for an appointment—can all be understood as manifestations of suffering.

I can understand why this comprehensive perspective can be hard to grasp, however. "Suffering"—the word often used in translations of the First Noble Truth—is a loaded term. When people first read or hear it, they tend to think that it refers only to extreme pain or chronic misery.

But *dukkha,* the word used in the *sutras,* is actually closer in meaning to terms more commonly used throughout the modern world, such as "uneasiness," "disease," "discomfort," and "dissatisfaction." Some Buddhist texts elaborate on its meaning through the use of a vivid analogy to a potter's wheel that sticks as it turns, making a sort of screeching sound. Other commentaries use an image of someone riding in a cart with a slightly broken wheel: every time the wheel rotates to the broken spot, the rider gets a jolt.

So, while suffering—or *dukkha*—does refer to extreme conditions, the term as used by the Buddha and later masters of Buddhist philosophy and practice is best understood as a pervasive feeling that *something isn't quite right*: that life could be better if circumstances were different; that we'd be happier if we were younger, thinner, or richer, in a relationship or out of a relationship. The list of miseries goes on and on. *Dukkha* thus embraces the entire spectrum of conditions, ranging from something as simple as an itch to more traumatic experiences of chronic pain or mortal illness. Maybe someday in the future the word *dukkha* will be accepted in many different languages and cultures, in the same way that the Sanskrit word *karma* has—offering us a broader understanding of a word that has often been translated as "suffering."

Just as having a doctor identify the symptoms is the first step in treating a disease, understanding *dukkha* as the basic condition of life is the first step to becoming free from discomfort or uneasiness. In fact, for some people, just hearing the First Noble Truth can, in itself, be a liberating experience. A long-term student of mine recently admitted that throughout his childhood and adolescence he'd always felt a little alienated from everyone around him. Other people seemed to know exactly the right thing to say and do. They were smarter than he was, they dressed better, and they seemed to get along with others without any effort. It seemed to him that everyone else in the world had been handed a "Happiness Handbook" at birth and he'd somehow been overlooked.

Later, when he took a college course in Eastern philosophy, he came across the Four Noble Truths, and his whole outlook began to change. He realized that he wasn't alone in his discomfort. In fact, awkwardness and alienation were experiences that had been shared by others for centuries. He could drop the whole sad story of missing out on the Happiness Handbook and just be exactly as he was. It didn't mean there wasn't work to do—but at least he could stop pretending to the outside world that he was really more together than he actually felt. He could begin working with his basic sense of inadequacy not as a lonely outsider, but as someone who had a common bond with the rest of humanity. It also meant that he was less likely to be caught off guard when he felt the particular ways suffering manifested for him come up—just as, for me, knowing that panic was around the corner took some of the sting out of it.

SURPRISE

> [Y]ou're walking down the street, on your way to meet a
> friend for dinner. You're already thinking about what you'd
> like to eat, savoring your hunger. Come around the corner
> and—oh no, a lion!
>
> —Robert Sapolsky, *Why Zebras Don't Get Ulcers*

Simply acknowledging the fact that, at any given moment, we may face some type of uneasy or uncomfortable experience constitutes the essential lesson of the First Noble Truth. But because this basic condition has so often been translated in stark language, I wanted to find some way to communicate it in terms that would be meaningful to people living in the modern world.

An analogy came to me during a recent teaching tour of North America, while I was taking a brisk, dusk-time walk through a park near the place where I was teaching. As I went through the park, I found myself engaging in a kind of "thought experiment"—a type of exercise of the imagination used by philosophers of the ancient world as well as scientists of the modern age to assist in understanding the nature of reality.

Some people, of course, may already be familiar with a few of the more historically famous thought experiments, such as the one conducted by Albert Einstein, which resulted in his development of the Special Theory of Relativity: the proposition that time and space aren't uniform aspects of reality, but are, instead, experiences that differ relative to the direction and speed in which a person is moving. Though the technological equipment necessary wasn't available at the time for Einstein to demonstrate his theory, more recent developments have shown his insights to be correct.

My own thought experiment wasn't concerned with the physical laws of motion but rather with the *psychological* aspects of *emotion*. I imagined what it would be like to pass through a wooded area like a park or a forest, engaged in thought or maybe listening to a portable music player and singing to myself. What might I experience if someone, deciding to play a joke, put on a very realistic bear costume and suddenly jumped out from behind a tree or building? My heart would begin to race, my skin would erupt in goose bumps, and my hair would stand on end. I'd probably scream in fright.

However, if someone had warned me about the joke, I wouldn't be quite as startled. I might even have an opportunity to give the joker a good scare in return—leaping out and screaming before he had a chance to jump out at me!

In the same way, if we understand *dukkha* or suffering as the basic condition of life, we're better prepared for the various discomforts we're likely to encounter along the way. Cultivating understanding of this sort is a bit like mapping the route of a journey. If we have a map, we have a better idea of where we are. If we don't have a map, we're likely to get lost.

TWO VIEWS OF SUFFERING

When this is born, that appears.
—*Sālistubhasūtra*, translated
by Maria Montenegro

As mentioned earlier, suffering operates on many different levels. Very early on, I was taught that in order to work with various kinds of suffering, it's essential to draw some distinctions among them.

One of the first, and most crucial, distinctions we can make is between what is often referred to as "natural" suffering and what I was taught to see as suffering of a "self-created" kind.

Natural suffering includes all the things we can't avoid in life. In classical Buddhist texts, these unavoidable experiences are often referred to as "The Four Great Rivers of Suffering." Categorized as

Birth, Aging, Illness, and Death, they are experiences that define the most common transitions in people's lives.

People have sometimes questioned me privately and in group teaching sessions as to why birth might be considered a form of suffering. "Surely," they say, "the beginning of a new life ought to be regarded as a moment of great joy." And in many respects, of course, it is: A new beginning is always an opportunity.

Birth, however, is considered an aspect of suffering for a couple of reasons. First of all, the transition from the protected environment of the womb (or an egg) into the wider world of sensory experience is considered—not only by Buddhist philosophers, but by many experts in the psychological, scientific, and health care fields—as something of a traumatic shift in experience. Many of us don't consciously recall the drama of this initial transition, but the experience of expulsion from an enclosed, protective environment apparently leaves a dramatic impression on the brain and body of a newborn.

Second, from the moment we're born, we become vulnerable to the other three Great Rivers of Suffering. The moment we're born, our "body clocks" start ticking. We grow older by the moment. As children, of course, most of us welcome this aspect of experience. I know I couldn't wait to grow up. I hated being bossed around by adults and couldn't wait to be able to make my own decisions. Now, of course, I realize that so many of the decisions I make have to be weighed quite carefully, because of their effects on others around me. And with every passing year, I start to feel more acutely the physical effects of aging. My joints have grown a little bit more stiff now and I'm more susceptible to fatigue and colds. I have to pay more attention to physical exercise.

As we proceed through life, too, we become susceptible to all sorts of diseases—the third Great River of Suffering. Some people are predisposed to allergies and other persistent ailments. Some succumb to severe illnesses such as cancer or AIDS. Others have spent years dealing with chronic physical pain. Many people I've met over the past several years suffer themselves or are dealing with friends or loved ones who are coping with catastrophic psycho-physiological diseases such as depression, bipolar disorder, addiction, and dementia.

The final of the Four Great Rivers of Suffering is death, the process through which the aspect of experience commonly referred to as consciousness becomes separated from the physical body. Tibetan texts such as *Bardo Thödol*—often referred to as "The Tibetan Book of the Dead," but more accurately translated as "Liberation Through Hearing"—describe this experience in extraordinary detail.

In many ways, death is a reversal of the birth process, a severing of the connections between physical, mental, and emotional aspects of experience. While birth is a process of becoming in a certain way "clothed" in physical, mental, and emotional swaddling, death is a process of being stripped of all the physical and psychological elements with which we have grown familiar. For this reason, the *Bardo Thödol* is often read aloud by a trained Buddhist master to a dying person, much in the way that last rites are administered by an ordained priest in Christian traditions as an aid to providing the dying with comfort through this often frightening transition.

As I've grown older and traveled more widely, I've begun to see that natural suffering includes far more categories than the ones listed in classical Buddhist texts. Earthquakes, floods, hurricanes, wildfires, and tidal waves wreak havoc on people's lives with increasing frequency. Over the past decade, I've heard and read about the tragic increase in murders perpetrated by children in high school and college classrooms. More recently, people have begun to speak much more openly to me about the devastation in their lives that has occurred through unexpectedly losing their jobs, their homes, or their relationships.

We don't have much choice in terms of our susceptibility to the experiences over which we have no control. But there is another category of pain, discomfort, *dukkha,* or whatever you want to call it: a virtually infinite variety of psychological tributaries that our minds spin around the people, events, and situations we encounter.

My father and other teachers helped me to think of this type of pain as "self-created": experiences that evolve from our interpretation of situations and events, such as impulsive anger or lingering resentment aroused by others who behave in ways we don't like, jealousy toward people who have more than we do, and paralyzing anxiety that occurs when there's no reason to be afraid.

Self-created suffering can take the form of the stories we tell ourselves, often deeply embedded in our unconsciousness, about not being good enough, rich enough, attractive enough, or secure in other ways. One of the more surprising forms of self-created suffering I've encountered over the past several years of teaching around the world involves physical appearance. People tell me how they just don't feel comfortable because their noses are too big, for instance, or their chins are too small. They feel self-conscious in the extreme, certain that everyone is looking at their big nose or their small chin. Even if they resort to plastic surgery to fix what they see as a problem, they still wonder if the surgeon did a good enough job; they're constantly checking out the results in a mirror and through other people's reactions.

One woman I met recently was convinced that one of her cheekbones was bigger than the other. I couldn't see it, but she was certain that this difference was real, and that it made her ugly—"deformed" is the way she put it, I think—in her own eyes and in the eyes of others. Every time she looked in the mirror, the "deformity" seemed more pronounced, and she was sure that everyone else noticed it, too. She monitored the way other people responded to her and became convinced that they were treating her as some sort of monster because of the difference in her cheekbones. As a result, she became very shy around other people and withdrew from contact, and her performance at work declined because she felt so hideous and insecure. It wasn't until she actually measured her cheekbones in a mirror and saw that that there was less than an eighth of an inch difference between them that she began to understand that the "deformity," and years of despair, fear, and self-hatred she'd experienced, were creations of her own mind.

So although self-created suffering is essentially a creation of the mind—as my own experience of anxiety showed me—it is no less intense than natural suffering. In fact, it can actually be quite a bit more painful. I remember quite vividly a monk I knew in India, whose friend, after being diagnosed with cancer in his leg, underwent an operation to amputate the affected limb. Shortly afterward, this monk began to feel such severe pains in his own leg that he couldn't move. He was taken to a hospital where a variety of scans and other tests were performed, none of which revealed any organic problem. Even after being presented with the results, the monk still felt intense pain in his leg, so the doctor began probing in another direction, asking about events in the monk's life that preceded the onset of the pain in his leg. Finally it came to light that the pain had started almost immediately after his friend's operation.

The doctor nodded thoughtfully and then began asking the monk about his reaction to seeing his friend. Gradually, the monk began to admit to feeling a great deal of fear, imagining what it would be like to feel the pain of having a leg removed and the difficulties he would have to face in learning how to walk with crutches and perform all sorts of other tasks that he used to take for granted. Without ever mentioning hypochondria, the doctor very gently led the monk through all the different scenarios he'd created in his own mind, until the monk realized how deeply the fear of pain—and the fear of fear—had affected him. Even as he was speaking, he felt the symptoms in his leg begin to fade, and the next day, he was able to walk out of the hospital, free of pain, and, most importantly, free of the *fear* that underlay the pain.

NOTHING PERSONAL

> *Be the chief, but never the lord.*
>
> —Lao Tzu, *The Way of Life,*
> translated by R.B. Blakney

The doctor's method of investigating the nature of the monk's pain echoed, in many ways, the skillfulness with which the Buddha presented the First Noble Truth. The Buddha didn't say to his listeners, "You are suffering," or "People suffer," or even "All creatures suffer." He merely said, "There is suffering"—offering it up as a general observation to be contemplated or reflected upon, rather than as some sort of final statement about the human condition that people might latch on to and identify with as a defining characteristic of their own lives. As if he were saying, "There is air" or "There are clouds," he presented suffering as a simple fact, undeniable, but not to be taken personally.

Psychologists I've talked to have suggested that introducing the First Noble Truth in this emotionally unthreatening fashion was an exceptionally perceptive means of acquainting us with the basic condition of suffering, in that it allows us to look at the ways in which it manifests in our experience a little bit more objectively. Instead of getting caught up in thinking, for example, "Why am I so lonely? It's not fair! I don't want to feel this. What can I do to get rid of it?"—trains of thought that lead us in the direction of judging ourselves or our circumstances or trying to reject or suppress our experience—we can take a step back and observe, "There is loneliness" or "There is anxiety" or "There is fear."

Approaching an uncomfortable experience with this type of impartial attitude is actually quite similar to the way in which my father taught me to just look at the distractions that came up for me every time I tried to meditate. "Don't judge them," he'd say. "Don't try to get rid of them. Just look." Of course, when I tried to do that, whatever was distracting me would vanish almost immediately. When I went back to my father to tell him about this problem, he smiled and said, "Oh, very good. Now you see."

I didn't—at least not then. I still had a few things to learn about the nature of suffering.

THE SUFFERING OF SUFFERING

[T]he pain of disease, malicious gossip etc. . . . constitutes
the misery of misery itself.

—Jamgon Kongtrul, *The Torch of Certainty,*
translated by Judith Hanson

Because suffering is such a broad term, many of the great masters who followed in the Buddha's footsteps expanded on his teachings of the First Noble Truth, dividing the variety of painful experiences into three basic categories.

The first is known as "The Suffering of Suffering," which can be described very briefly as the immediate and direct experience of any sort of pain or discomfort. A very simple example might be the pain you experience if you accidentally cut your finger. Included within this category, as well, would be the various aches and pains associated with illness, which can vary in intensity from headaches, stuffy noses, and sore throats to the more intense kinds of pain experienced by people who suffer from chronic or fatal diseases. The discomforts that come with aging, like arthritis, rheumatism, weakening limbs, and heart and respiratory distress, would also be regarded as manifestations of the Suffering of Suffering. So would the pain one experiences as the victim of an accident or a natural disaster—broken bones, severe burns, or trauma to internal organs.

Most of the examples described above relate to what was defined earlier as natural suffering. But the pain and discomfort associated with the Suffering of Suffering extends, as well, to the psychological and emotional dimensions of self-created suffering.

The terror and anxiety that welled up in me throughout my childhood, though they didn't necessarily have an organic cause, were certainly immediate and direct. Other intense emotions like anger, jealousy, embarrassment, the hurt that follows when someone says or does something unkind, and the grief that follows the loss of a loved one are equally vivid experiences of this sort of suffering, as are more persistent psychological disturbances like depression, loneliness, and low self-esteem.

The emotional manifestations of the Suffering of Suffering aren't necessarily extreme or persistent. They can be quite simple. For example, I was speaking not long ago with someone who'd run from her office to the bank on her lunch hour, only to find a long line at the teller window. "I wanted to scream," she told me, "because I knew I had to get back for an important meeting, so I only had a limited amount of time. I didn't scream, of course; I'm not that type of person. Instead, I just pulled out the presentation for the meeting and started going over it, glancing between the pages, my watch, and the line that just didn't seem to move. I couldn't believe the amount of resentment I felt at all the people ahead of me, and at the bank teller—who appeared, to give her credit, to be trying to remain patient while dealing with an apparently difficult customer. I can laugh at the situation now, but I was *still* resentful when I got back to the office, without having time for lunch, and the feeling didn't lift until the meeting was over, and I dashed out for a sandwich to bring back to my desk."

THE SUFFERING OF CHANGE

Cast aside concerns for worldly activities.

—The Ninth Gyalwa Karmapa,
Mahāmudrā: The Ocean of Definitive Meaning,
translated by Elizabeth M. Callahan

The second category of suffering, as it was explained to me, is much more subtle. Referred to as "The Suffering of Change," this kind of suffering is often described in terms of deriving satisfaction, comfort, security, or pleasure from objects or situations that are bound to change. Suppose, for example, you get a new car, a television set, or a shiny new computer with all the latest components. For a while, you're ecstatic. You love how smoothly the car rides, how fast you can pull away when the traffic light turns green, how easily the press of a button automatically warms the seats on a cold winter morning. The picture on your new, flat-screen TV is so clear and bright, with definition so amazing that you can pick out details you never saw before. That new computer lets you run ten different programs with incredible speed. But after a while, the novelty of whatever it is you bought wears off. Maybe the car breaks down; somebody you know gets a TV with a bigger, clearer screen; the computer crashes—or a new model comes out that has even more features and more power. You might think, "I wish I'd waited."

Or perhaps it's not a thing that makes you happy, but a situation. You fall in love and the world is filled with rainbows; every time you think of the other person, you can't keep from smiling. Or you get a new job or promotion, and oh, everyone you're working with now is so great, and the money you're making—finally you can pay off your debts, maybe buy a new house, or really start saving. After a while the glow wears off, though, doesn't it? You start to see flaws in the person who seemed so perfect just a few months ago. That new job demands more time and energy than you imagined and the salary, well, it's not as great as you imagined. There isn't really much left over for savings after taxes are taken out and once you've started paying off your debts.

This explanation of the Suffering of Change is close, but it misses the point. The dissatisfaction or disenchantment experienced when the novelty wears off or the situation starts to fall apart is actually the Suffering of Suffering. The Suffering of Change stems, more accurately, from the *attachment to the pleasure derived from getting what we want:* be it a relationship, a job, a good grade on an exam, or a shiny new car.

Unfortunately, the pleasure derived from external sources is, by nature, temporary. Once it wears off, the return to our "normal" state seems less bearable by comparison. So we seek it again, maybe in another relationship, another job, or another object. Again and again, we seek pleasure, comfort, or relief in objects and situations that can't possibly fulfill our high hopes and expectations.

The Suffering of Change, then, could be understood as a type of addiction, a never-ending search for a lasting "high" that is just out of reach. In fact, according to neuroscientists I've spoken with, the high we feel simply from the anticipation of getting what we want is linked to the production of dopamine, a chemical in the brain that generates, among other things, sensations of pleasure. Over time, our brains and our bodies are motivated to repeat the activities that stimulate the production of dopamine. We literally get hooked on anticipation.

Tibetan Buddhist texts liken this type of addictive behavior to "licking honey off a razor." The initial sensation may be sweet, but the underlying effect is quite damaging. Seeking satisfaction in others or in external objects or events reinforces a deep and often unacknowledged belief that we, as we are, are not entirely complete; that we need something beyond ourselves in order to experience a sense of wholeness or security or stability. The Suffering of Change is perhaps best summed up as a conditional view of ourselves. *I'm fine as long as I have this or that going for me. My job is demanding, but at least I have a great relationship (or my health or my looks or a wonderful family).*

PERVASIVE SUFFERING

> *A single hair lying on the palm of the hand*
> *Causes discomfort and suffering if it gets into the eye.*
>
> —Rājaputra Yashomitra, *Commentary on the "Treasury of*
> *Abhidharma,"* translated by Elizabeth M. Callahan

The foundation of the first two categories of suffering—as well as the kinds of suffering that can be described as natural and self-created—is known as Pervasive Suffering. Of itself, this type of suffering is not overtly painful nor does it involve the sort of addictive pleasure-seeking associated with the Suffering of Change. It might best be described as a fundamental restlessness, a kind of itch persisting just below the level of conscious awareness.

Think of it this way: you're sitting in a very comfortable chair during a meeting or lecture, or just watching TV. But no matter how comfortable the chair is, at some point you feel the urge to move, to rearrange your backside, or to stretch your legs. That's Pervasive Suffering. You could find yourself in the most wonderful circumstances, but eventually a twinge of discomfort plucks at you and whispers, "Mmm, not quite right. Things could be better if . . ."

Where does that itch, that subtle twinge of dissatisfaction, come from?

Very simply put, everything in our experience is always changing. The world around us, our bodies, our thoughts and feelings—even our thoughts *about* our thoughts and feelings—are in constant flux, a progressive and ceaseless interplay of causes and conditions that create certain effects, which *themselves* become the causes and conditions that give rise to still other effects. In Buddhist terms, this constant change is known as *impermanence*. In many of his teachings the Buddha compared this movement to the tiny changes that occur in the flow of a river. Viewed from a distance, the moment by moment changes are difficult to perceive. It's only when we step up to the riverbank and take a really close look that we can see the tiny changes in wave patterns—the shifts of sand, silt, and debris, and the movement of fish and other creatures who inhabit the water—and begin to appreciate the incredible variety of changes going on moment by moment.

Impermanence occurs on many levels, some of which are clear to see. For example, we wake up one morning to discover that the empty lot down the road has become a busy construction site, full of the noise and bustle of digging the foundation, pouring concrete, erecting steel beams for the structure, and so on. Before long the skeleton of a building has been raised, and another team of people are busy laying water pipes and gas lines and running electrical wires throughout the structure. Later still, other teams come to put the walls and windows in, and maybe do a bit of land-scaping, planting trees, grass, and gardens. Finally, instead of an empty lot, there's a whole building full of people coming and going.

This obvious level of change is referred to in Buddhist teachings as *gross continuous impermanence*. We can see the transformation of the empty lot, and though we may not like the new building—maybe it blocks our view, or if it's a big commercial building, we might be disturbed by the increase in the amount of traffic in front of the building—the change doesn't take us by surprise.

Gross continuous impermanence can also be observed in the change of seasons, at least in certain parts of the world. For a few months, it's very cold and snow covers the ground. A few months later there are buds on trees and early flowers start springing from the ground. After a time, the buds turn into leaves and fields and gardens burst with many different plants and flowers. When autumn comes, the flowers wither and the leaves on the trees may start turning red, yellow, or orange. Then winter returns, and the leaves and flowers disappear and the air turns cold; sometimes there's snow and sometimes ice covers trees like a coating of pure glass.

While the effects of gross continuous impermanence are readily apparent, they actually arise from another type of continuous change, which the Buddha described as *subtle impermanence*, a shifting of conditions that occurs "behind the scenes" as it were, on such a deep level that it barely, if ever, approaches our awareness.

One way to understand the workings of subtle impermanence is to consider the way we think of time.

In general, we tend to conceive of time in terms of three categories: past, present, and future. If we look at these three cate-gories in terms of years, we can say that there is last year, this year, and next year. But last year has already faded and next year hasn't arrived yet: essentially, they're concepts, ideas we have about time.

That leaves us with *this* year.

But a year is made up of months, isn't it? This can get a little con-fusing for me because most Western calendars are made up of twelve months, while the Tibetan calendar sometimes includes an extra, thirteenth month! But let's use the Western calendar as an example, and agree, for the moment, that we're in the middle of the sixth month. Nearly six months of the year have already passed and six lie ahead. So now what we call the present has been reduced in scope from this *year* to this *month*. But a month is made up of a fixed number of days—in the Western calendar, usually thirty or thirty-one. So if it's June 15, half of June has passed and the other half has yet to be. Now the present is only this *day*. But this day is composed of twenty-four hours; and if it's noon, half of the day has passed while the other half hasn't arrived.

We can keep breaking down the passage of time further and fur-ther—into the sixty minutes that make up an hour; the sixty sec-onds that make up a minute; the milliseconds that make up a second; the nanoseconds that make up each millisecond; on and on as far as scientists can measure. Those tiny bits of time are al-ways moving, flying away from us. The future becomes the present and the present becomes the past before we're even consciously aware of what's happening. Neuroscientists I've spoken with have measured a half-second gap—called the "attentional blink"—between the moment our sensory organs register a visual stimulus and pass on the signals to the brain and the moment in which we consciously identify those signals and consolidate them in short-term memory.[1] By the time we even register the idea "now," it's already "then."

No matter how much we'd like to, we can't stop time or the changes it brings. We can't "rewind" our lives to an earlier point or "fast-forward" to some future place. But we can learn to accept impermanence, make friends with it, and even begin to consider the possibility of change as a type of mental and emotional bodyguard.

THE BREATH OF CHANGE

Breath is life.

—Sogyal Rinpoche, *The Tibetan Book of Living and Dying*
edited by Patrick Gaffney and Andrew Harvey

Some people can understand impermanence just by contemplating the teachings on the First Noble Truth. For others, understanding doesn't come so easily—or it remains a concept, somewhat mysterious and abstract. Fortunately, the Buddha and the great masters who followed in his footsteps provided a number of simple exercises that can help us get in touch with the subtle level of change in a direct and nonthreatening way. The simplest of all, which can be practiced anytime, anywhere, involves bringing attention to the changes that happen to the body as we breathe.

Begin by sitting with your spine straight and body relaxed. If it's more comfortable, you can lie down. You can keep your eyes open

[1]See H. A. Sleeger, et al, "Mental Training Affects Distribution of Limited Brain Resources," *PLoS Biology*, June 2007, vol. 5, no. 6, e138.

or closed (although I wouldn't recommend closing your eyes if you're driving or walking down the street). Just breathe in and out naturally through your nose. And as you do, gently bring your attention to the changes in your body as you breathe, especially the expansion and contraction of your lungs and the rising and falling of the muscles in the abdominal region. Don't worry about concentrating too hard, thinking "I've *got* to watch my breath . . . I've *got* to watch my breath." Just let your mind rest in bare awareness of the changes occurring as you breathe in and out. Don't worry, either, if you find your mind wandering as you continue the exercise—that is simply another lesson in impermanence. If you find yourself thinking about something that happened yesterday, or daydreaming about tomorrow, gently bring your attention back to the changes in the body as you breathe. Continue this exercise for about a minute.

When the minute is up, review what you noticed about the changes in your body. Don't judge the experience or try to explain it. Just review what you noticed. You may have felt other things aside from the rising and falling of your abdomen or the expansion and contraction of your lungs. You may have been more aware of the breath flowing in and out of your nostrils. That's okay. You may have become aware of hundreds of different thoughts, feelings, and sensations, or of being carried away by distractions. That's great. Why? Because you're taking the time to observe the constant changes occurring on a subtle level without resisting them.

If you continue this practice once a day or a few times a day, you'll find yourself becoming aware of more changes, on subtler and subtler levels. Gradually, impermanence will become like an old friend, nothing to get upset about, nothing to resist. Over time, you may discover that you can carry this awareness into other situations—at work perhaps, or while waiting at the grocery store, or at the bank, or even while eating lunch or dinner. Just bringing yourself back to your breath is an effective way of "tuning in" to the fullness of the present moment and orienting yourself to the subtle changes going on inside and around you. This in turn will provide you with the opportunity to see things more clearly and act from a psychological state of greater openness and balance. Whenever disturbing thoughts or sensations arise—or if you happen to be caught off guard by a wax figure suddenly coming to life—the situation will act as a kind of reminder of the basic fact that impermanence simply *is*.

So why does it seem so personal?

To answer this question, we need to look at the Second of the Four Noble Truths.

3

THE POWER OF PERSPECTIVE

It is impossible to guard one's training without guarding the wandering mind.

—Śāntideva, *The Bodhicaryāvatāra,*
translated by Kate Crosby and Andre Skilton

SEVERAL YEARS AGO I was walking down a street in India, where many of the roads are still paved with stones. I'd set out in a hurry without putting on my sandals—a decision I soon regretted, because the sensation of walking barefoot down a stony road was, to say the least, uncomfortable. Not long afterwards I happened to mention this experience to an Indian doctor.

"Oh, very good!" he replied.

When I asked what he meant, he explained that, according to several ancient medical systems, applying pressure to various points along the soles of the feet stimulated activity in various organs and systems, thus promoting overall health. People who have some familiarity with foot reflexology are aware of the potential benefits associated with the practice, but for me, it was a novel idea. After listening to the doctor's explanation I started going barefoot more often. To my surprise, instead of discomfort I began to feel pleasure in the sensation of stones underfoot.

Why?

The stones hadn't changed. My feet hadn't changed. The physical act of walking hadn't changed.

As I thought about it, I realized that the only aspect of the experience that had changed was my perspective. Previously I'd simply assumed that walking on stones would be painful. When the doctor offered a different way of looking at the situation, that alternate possibility opened the way for a transformation of experience.

A CLOSER LOOK

> *The way we experience things is simply the display of our minds.*
>
> —Khenpo Karthar Rinpoche,
> *The Instructions of Gampopa,*
> translated by Lama Yeshe Gyamtso

Although I'd used the same basic principle of shifting my perspective in working with the thoughts and emotions that had troubled me as a child, I hadn't really applied it to very many situations involving physical discomfort. It came as something of a shock to realize how deeply I'd associated my physical body with the idea of "me."

But there was an even more important lesson to be gained from this incident, one that has influenced the way I look at any troubling or uncomfortable situation. If I hadn't felt the discomfort in the first place or if I'd surrendered to it or tried to resolve it in an ordinary way—for instance, by making an effort to remember to put on my sandals every time I left my room—I wouldn't have seen that subtle layer of conditioning.

Since then, I've begun to develop a greater appreciation for those moments in which I experience pain or discomfort. Each one is a seed of deeper understanding, an opportunity to get to know my mind a little bit better, and to observe ideas about myself and the world around me that I didn't even know I had.

I don't mean to suggest that whenever I face a problem or feel irritation or discomfort I put on some sort of Buddhist detective cap and start rummaging through my mind asking, "Hmm, what's the perspective here . . . What am I not seeing? Oh, there it is! Now let me substitute a new one." That's just a sneaky attempt to get rid of an uncomfortable situation, which ends up reinforcing the habit of seeing challenges as enemies to be conquered or "bosses" to be pacified.

The actual process involves simply staying with the situation and looking at it directly. Approaching experience in this way allows a bit of space to spontaneously open up around it, allowing us to see it in a larger context. If there's a mind that can look at an experience, logically it follows that that mind is larger than the experience itself. In that split second of recognition, it becomes possible to catch a glimpse of the mind's infinite grandeur: to see it, as my father and other teachers described, as an endless ocean in which each moment of experience is nothing more than one among a series of waves—now rising, now falling—never separate from a limitless expanse.

This glimpse also provides a working basis for comprehending the Second Noble Truth, often translated as the "origin" or "cause" of suffering. Our normal tendency is to assign the cause of suffering to circumstances or conditions. According to the Second Noble Truth, however, the cause of suffering lies not in events or circumstances, but in the way we perceive and interpret our experience as it unfolds.

One very striking example of the way in which perspective affects experience is drawn from the practice of devotees of certain Eastern religions, who will set the tips of their fingers on fire as a means of relieving the suffering of beings who experience a deeper and darker pain than many of us can imagine. The joy they have reported experiencing in making offerings of their own bodies more than offsets whatever pain they feel.

On a somewhat less extreme level, it can be said that, in general, people don't like to have their bodies kneaded or pressed, especially in areas where knots in the muscles are particularly tight. And yet they will pay for a massage, anticipating that the kneading and pressing will ultimately relieve various aches and pains and help them feel better in the long run. They'll make an appointment for pain!

I recently heard a story about a woman in Taiwan who, walking down the street with a couple of friends, felt her sock become tangled up in her shoe, causing her some pain and discomfort. "Stop!" she shouted. "I've got to fix this. The pain is unbearable." Ironically, she was on her way to an appointment with a foot reflexologist, and when she got there she demanded, "Press harder! I'm paying a lot of money for this and I want to get my money's worth!"

I had to laugh. One moment, she was experiencing pressure on her foot that seemed unendurable, and half an hour later she was demanding more! Her response to the same basic situation changed wildly according to her interpretation and expectations.

But where do these interpretations come from, and why do they affect us so deeply?

THE RELATIVITY OF PERSPECTIVE

These forms we see with our physical eyes we tend to appraise in various ways.

—Khenchen Thrangu Rinpoche,
The Ninth Karmapa's Ocean of Definitive Meaning,
translated by Lama Yeshe Gyamtso

As we go about our lives, we depend for the most part on our capacity to make distinctions. Some of them seem very direct and simple: right and left, tall and short, loud and quiet, feet and hands, night and day. Some require a bit more discernment. *Is this piece of fruit overripe or not ripe enough? Is this a reasonable price for something or could I find the same thing cheaper at another store?* Some require even deeper consideration—an experience I find especially common among parents who wonder whether they're being too harsh or too lenient in disciplining their children, and also among people concerned about angry exchanges or differences of opinion in relationships with their spouses or partners: *Did we say what we said or do what we did because we were having a bad day or out of a more deep-seated disagreement?* I've also heard questions of a similar sort from those seeking counsel regarding people and events in their workplace. *Am I judging this person unsympathetically? Am I working too hard and not taking enough time for myself or my family?*

The important thing to bear in mind is that all distinctions are fundamentally *relative*—ideas, judgments, and sensations are based on comparison.

To use a very simple example, if you place a four-inch glass beside a six-inch glass, the four-inch glass is going to be shorter than the six-inch one. But if you place a six-inch glass next to an eight-inch glass, the six-inch glass—which was previously seen as "tall"—is now going to be "short." Similarly, left makes sense only in relation to right, night makes sense only in comparison to day, and warm makes sense only in comparison to cold. That's a short course in what is often referred to in Buddhist teachings as *relative reality*: a level of experience defined by distinctions.

As I understand through discussions with various scientists, the capacity to make distinctions evolved as a survival tool. There is, inarguably, an advantage to distinguishing, say, between plants or fruits that are poisonous and sources of food that are nourishing. Likewise, it would be quite useful to distinguish between something to eat and something that might eat us!

Human beings respond in complicated ways to this distinction-making process, which may be understood in both biological and psychological terms.

From a strictly biological point of view, any act of perception requires three essential elements: organs of sensation—like the eye, the ear, the nose, the tongue, and the skin; an object of sensation—such as, say, a flower; and the capacity to process and respond to the signals we receive from our sense organs. The sense organs, the areas of the brain, and the links that connect them are made up primarily of cells known as *neurons*. The human brain is made up of billions of neurons, many of which are organized to form structures related to learning, memory, and emotion. The interaction between these structures can be very complicated.

Let's say you're looking at a flower: a red rose, to be specific. That's the object—or what, in scientific terms, is referred to as a *stimulus*. Now when you look at the rose, the cells in your eye first notice this thing made up of a bunch of red things that are sort of round at the top and sort of pointed at the bottom, where they connect with a long green thing that may have green roundish things poking out of it along with some darker, pointy things. The image is transmitted through a group of cells that constitute a kind of fiber or cord that make up the *optic nerve,* which sends visual information from the eye to the *visual cortex,* an area in the brain dedicated to organizing stimuli received through the sense of sight.

Upon receiving this visual stimulus, the visual cortex sends an "instant message" to the area of the brain known as the *thalamus,* a group of cells located near the very center of the brain, where many of the messages from the senses are "decoded" before being sent to other areas of the brain. Interestingly, the word *thalamus* is an ancient Greek term meaning "bedroom"—a place where private conversations are often known to occur.

Once the messages from the visual cortex are passed to the thalamus, they're sent in several directions. One set is sent to the *limbic system,* a layer of the brain primarily responsible for distinguishing between pain and pleasure, determining emotional responses, and providing a foundation for learning and memory.

Two important structures in this area of the brain play particularly significant roles in interpreting these messages and the memories we make of them. One is the *amygdala,* a small, almond-shaped group of neurons that determine the emotional content of experience. If you were pricked by one of those "dark, pointy things," for example, you may likely respond to that "red thing made up of a bunch of red things" as "bad" or "unpleasant." The other is the *hippocampus*, which is a kind of storehouse for the spatial and temporal elements of memory. It provides the context or meaning for experience, enabling us to remember, for example, where and when we saw a rose for the first time.

Simultaneously the intimate conversation gathered in the bedroom of the thalamus is passed on to the *neocortex*, the outermost layer of the brain widely understood by neuroscientists as an area devoted primarily to analytical functions. This is the area of the brain in which we begin to learn how to name things, discern patterns, and formulate concepts—where we define "the red thing made up of a bunch of red things" as a rose. It's also the area that modulates the memories and emotional responses generated in the limbic region, tamping down some and heightening others.

Though lengthy to describe, all of this communication between the thousands of cells that make up our sense organs and the various neuronal structures in the brain occurs in a fraction of a second, less time than it takes to snap our fingers. And the brain responds almost immediately, prompting the release of chemicals like cortisol, adrenaline, dopamine, and endorphins to course through our bodies to slow or speed our heart rate and shift our mood. At the same time, a series of links is established among sense organs, brain-structures, vital organs, and glands—a kind of instant messaging network that, put very simply, creates an internal "map" of a red rose.

In other words, we're not really seeing the rose itself, but rather a concept of it. This concept is often conditioned by a broad range of factors, including the circumstances surrounding our initial experience, the memories and expectations stored in various parts of the brain, modifications that may occur through later experience—and, perhaps most importantly, the distinction between the experiencer (me) and what is experienced (the rose).

The distinction of "me" as an entity inherently separate from, for example, a rose, is itself an internal image that emerges from the interactions among various neuronal structures and other bodily systems. This image may be quite vague very early in life. As we mature, however, our internalized sense of "me" as something distinct from "not me" becomes more vivid, as do distinctions such as "pleasant" and "unpleasant," and "desirable" and "undesirable." We also distinguish a sort of "neutral" zone, in which we haven't decided how we relate to our experience. Just as some people organize files, papers, photographs, and other things by putting them in different boxes, we arrange our experiences in conceptual "boxes."

From my discussions with people trained in various scientific disciplines, it's clear there are some differences of opinion as to how, when, and why these boxes emerge. There does seem to be some agreement among modern schools of thought, however, that the "me" box begins to develop at birth, when an infant is separated from the body of his or her mother and begins to experience life as an individual being, facing an internal and external environment that is not altogether predictable.

As infants, we're driven by a need for comfort, particularly in the form of food or warmth, as well as by a resistance to experiences of discomfort, like being hungry, cold, or wet. Sometimes we're comforted; sometimes we're not. The "me" box may not be very solid or consistent—or even expressible except in terms of crying, burping, gurgling, or grinning—but inherent in pleasant and unpleasant experiences is the possibility of defining a "not-me" box, along with "good," "bad," and other boxes.

Later, during the stage that many parents describe as the "terrible twos," when children begin to assert an independent identity—more often than not by saying "no"—these different boxes appear to have taken a more solid, definite shape. The potential for other boxes to emerge is already set in motion.

KILLING BUTTERFLIES

> *Beings think "I" at first and cling to self;*
> *They think of "mine" and are attached to things.*
> —Chandrakirti, *Introduction to the Middle Way,*
> translated by the Padmakara Translation Group

Centuries before the development of Western science, the Buddha arrived at an understanding that suffering originates in the mind—in the "eye," so to speak, "of the beholder." Though the terms he used may differ from those of modern-day biologists, neuroscientists, and psychologists, the insights he offered are remarkably similar.

According to the early written presentations of the Buddha's teachings on the Second Noble Truth, *dukkha* arises from a basic mental condition referred to in Pali as *taṇhā*, or "craving." The students who translated the early Pali transcripts into Sanskrit defined the cause as *trishna*, or "thirst." When the teachings were brought to Tibet, the cause was translated as *dzinpa*, or "grasping."

In their own ways, each of these three terms reflects a fundamental yearning for permanence or stability—or, looked at in another way, an attempt to deny or ignore impermanence. The most basic of these yearnings is the tendency, often described in Buddhist texts as *ignorance*, to mistake "self," "other," "subject," "object," "good," "bad," and other relative distinctions as independently, inherently existing. On a very simple level, ignorance could be described as thinking that the label on a bottle of hot sauce *is* the hot sauce.

From the conception of people, places, and things as inherently solid and real arise two similarly powerful urges. The first, commonly referred to as *desire,* is a craving to acquire or keep whatever we determine as pleasant. The second, known as *aversion*, is a pull in the opposite direction, to avoid or eliminate things we define as unpleasant.

Collectively, ignorance, desire, and aversion are referred to in Buddhist writings as "The Three Poisons," habits of relating to experience that are so deeply rooted that they cloud or "poison" the mind. Individually and in combination, they give rise to innumerable other attitudes and emotions—for example, pride, perfectionism, low self-esteem, or self-hatred; the jealousy we feel when a coworker gets a promotion we think we deserve; or the lump of grief and hopelessness that overwhelm us when dealing with an ill or aging parent. Accordingly, some Buddhist teachings refer to these attitudes and emotions as "afflictions" or "obscurations," because they limit the ways in which we interpret our experience— which, in turn, inhibits our potential to think, feel, and act. Once we develop a sense of "me" and "not me," we begin to relate to our experience in terms of "mine" and "not mine"; "what I have" and "what I don't have"; and "what I want" and "what I don't want."

Imagine, for example, that you're driving down the road in your own, worn-out old car, and pass a fancy new car—a Mercedes or a Rolls-Royce—that's just been dented in an accident. You might feel a little sorry for the owner, but you wouldn't necessarily feel any attachment to the car. A few months later, finding yourself in a position to trade in your old car, you visit a used auto lot—and there's a Mercedes or Rolls-Royce available at an incredible price! It's actually the same car you saw dented in an accident a few months earlier, but as soon as you sign the contract, it doesn't matter. The car is *yours* now—and as you drive it home, a pebble cracks the windshield. Tragedy! *My* car is ruined. *I'm* going to have to pay to get it fixed.

It's the same car dented in an accident a few months earlier, and you may not have felt much about it one way or another as you drove by. But now it's *your* car, and if the windshield is cracked, you experience anger, frustration, and maybe a little fear.

So why not just stop? Why not just let go of the poisons and their "offspring"?

If it were that easy, of course, we'd all be buddhas before we reached the end of this sentence!

According to the Buddha's teachings and commentaries by other masters, the Three Poisons and all the other mental and emotional habits that arise from them are not in themselves the causes of suffering. Rather, suffering arises from *attachment* to them, which is the closest you can get to the essential meaning of the Tibetan word *dzinpa*. As mentioned earlier, this word is often interpreted as "grasping," but I've also heard it translated as "fixation," which I think captures more closely the deeper significance of the term. *Dzinpa* is an attempt to fix in time and place that which is constantly moving and changing.

"That's like killing butterflies!" a student of mine recently exclaimed.

When I asked her what she meant, she described how some

people make a hobby of capturing butterflies, killing them, and pinning their bodies in glass or plastic display cases for the sheer pleasure of looking at their collection or showing them off to their friends.

"Such beautiful, delicate creatures," she said sadly. "They're meant to fly. If they don't fly, they're not really butterflies anymore, are they?"

In a way, she was right.

When we become fixed in our perceptions, we lose our ability to fly.

MIRROR, MIRROR

All living beings, the contents of this world, are impermanent.

—Jamgon Kongtrul, *The Torch of Certainty,*
translated by Judith Hanson

The intensity of suffering caused by strong attachment to a set of beliefs or perceptions was vividly demonstrated to me through an encounter with an elderly woman who came to visit me in the United States a few years back. As soon as she sat down, she started to cry.

"It's okay," I told her. "When you've calmed down, you can tell me what's wrong."

We waited a few moments while she composed herself. Finally she said, "I don't want to be old. When I look in the mirror, I see all these wrinkles and I hate them. I hate them so much, the other day I broke my mirror. So of course I had to go out and buy another one. But when I look in it, all I can see are the wrinkles and it drives me crazy. I get so angry and depressed I don't know what to do."

I have to admit, I was a little surprised by her outburst. My grandmother had had a lot of wrinkles, but I thought they made her face all the more beautiful—so soft and gentle, full of wisdom, and always smiling. I didn't say this directly, of course. When someone is experiencing pain, probably the worst thing we can do is say something like, "Well, that's just your perception. Change your perception and your experience will change." If one of my teachers had said anything like that to me when I was bound up in my own anxiety and fear, I don't think it would have made any sense to me and I might have ended up feeling more alone and bewildered than I already felt. What I needed during my own struggles was an understanding that I was facing a dilemma that all people—all living creatures, in one way or another—experience: a profound and penetrating desire to survive, to live and to flourish, and maybe to experience some moments of peace.

I'm grateful to my father and my other teachers for taking me through this process. They urged me to just look at what I was experiencing—and to comprehend through simply looking that thoughts, emotions, judgments, and sensations come and go. In doing so, they brought home in a very practical way the brilliance of the Buddha's teachings on the Four Noble Truths. He could have skipped the Second Noble Truth altogether—going from the first, the Truth of Suffering, to the third, the Truth of Cessation. Instead, he offered an explanation that would help us to face and work with the causes and conditions that create whatever hardships we experience in this life. At the same time, the Second Noble Truth emphasizes that we are not alone in facing challenges. In one way or another, attachment to our perceptions of who or what we are, what we want or need, and what we don't want or need, is common to all living creatures.

Following the example of my teachers, I began talking to the woman so pained by her wrinkles about impermanence and how it is the basic condition we all face. If we can accept it, then we can actually see that there are some benefits to the changes, overt and subtle, we undergo throughout the course of life.

"When you fixate on what you were like and what you were capable of doing when you were young," I told her, "you won't be able to see some of the advantages to growing old. Think about the things that you can do now that you couldn't do when you were young. Think of the perspective your experience has brought you. You might also remember," I added, "points in your life when you were young and you couldn't wait to be older, to enjoy the opportunities that a wiser, more experienced, and respected person enjoys. If you fixate only on the gross levels of change, you won't see the benefits of the subtler changes. When I was younger, I couldn't wait to get old. I'd be free to do what I want and be more stable. Nobody could tell me what to do."

A year later, when I was passing through the United States again, she came for another visit. This time, she was relaxed and smiling, and after she sat down, she announced that she hadn't broken any mirrors since our last meeting.

"I realized after our talk," she explained, "that time wasn't my enemy; age wasn't my enemy. My own fixation was my enemy. When I looked in the mirror, all I saw was what I thought other people were seeing—an old woman, unattractive and useless. And I started acting that way too, so of course people started treating me as old and useless. It became a vicious cycle.

"But when I started thinking about the experience I'd gained over the years, I actually started feeling a little proud of my wrinkles. Each one was like a badge of honor, a crisis survived, a test passed. I started looking at other people my age, thinking, 'Yes, we've all gone through a lot. And there's more to come, little changes and big ones.' I won't say I jump out of bed every morning looking forward to the changes. I'm a little old for jumping," she laughed. "But I find myself paying more attention to my life, to the moment, you might say. Because that's all I have, isn't it? The moment. And there's a lot more going on in this one moment than I ever thought."

I was impressed. With very little guidance, this woman had come to terms with the attachment to an idea of herself, the principal cause of the discomfort that underlies so much of human experience. She'd faced it and learned from it, and in so doing gained a deeper appreciation of her life.

That is the essential lesson of the Second Noble Truth. Acknowledging that all conditions are bound to change, we can approach each moment with a bit more clarity and confidence, relaxing into it rather than resisting it or being overwhelmed by it. We don't have to be bossed around by our experiences. Neither do we have to fight or flee from them as "enemies." We have the potential to look at our experiences and recognize, "This is what's happening now, at this moment. The next moment will bring another experience, and the moment after that will bring another."

Resistance to these moment-by-moment changes is one of the best ways I know to explain in modern terms the fixation which the Buddha and later teachers describe as the cause of the broad range of suffering and discomfort encompassed by the term *dukkha*.

CONDITIONS

Even a tiny spark of fire/Can set alight a mountain of hay.
—Patrul Rinpoche, *The Words of My Perfect Teacher,*
translated by the Padmakara Translation Group

Attachment to the poisons may be considered the immediate cause of suffering, but just as a seed typically requires some combination of soil, water, and sunlight in order to ripen, the various afflictions develop in different ways according to the complex interaction of conditions that vary from individual to individual. Many of these conditions arise from specific personal experiences, the family environment in which we were raised, the influence of the cultures in which we live, as well as genetic factors that are only now beginning to be understood by experts in the fields of biology and neuroscience. Such factors may be considered the soil, water, and sunlight of our individual lives.

Among many Asian cultures, for example, signs of age are acknowledged as tokens of respect: a widespread cultural acknowledgment that long life confers some type of wisdom derived through experience. In many of the Western countries I've visited, signs of age appear to represent some kind of loss, frailty, or being "out of touch." In India, where I have spent a great deal of my life, a large belly, a round face, and a double or even triple chin are considered by many as signs of health and success and wealth. Yet among many of the people I've met in Western cultures these same physical characteristics are often considered signs of ill health.

In many cultures—Eastern as well as Western—the social situation into which you're born may be considered a sign of strength or weakness, and may have an effect on how a person views him- or herself and is viewed by others. The Buddha, for example, was born to the *kshatriya* or "warrior" class, and was raised with a great many privileges denied to many other members of Indian society of his era. Abandoning his position and privileges, he took an important step toward acknowledging the influence familial and cultural conditions have in determining our perception of ourselves.

How?

He simply rode away. I can't say what was going through his mind as he left all those privileges behind, but I suspect there may have been a sense of freedom—a feeling of release from the expectations that bound him.

Children born in the same family are sometimes subtly, sometimes openly compared against each other. One person I encountered on a recent trip to Canada described this situation: "My older brother—the firstborn—was always considered the golden boy," he said. "He could do no wrong in my father's eyes. My father spent hours with him, teaching him how to throw a baseball, fix a car engine, and drive a boat. When my time came to learn these things, my dad would often grumble, 'Why can't you be as smart as your brother? You're never going to do this right.'

"I was lucky in some ways, though," he continued. "My mother was always there behind the scenes, telling me that I was smart in other ways. 'You've got a good math brain,' she'd say.

"Ultimately, I became an accountant and my brother became a mechanic. Looked at from the outside, I have a much more comfortable life than he does: a well-paying job, a large house, two nice cars, and the ability to send my daughters to piano and dance lessons. But I've never been able to escape the feeling that I'm somehow *less-than,* that everything I do at work and for my family is an attempt to be the 'golden boy' I never was as a child.

"I love my brother and we get along very well. But I still feel a little jealous of him and that jealousy extends to other people I work with. I'm always worried about pleasing my supervisors and I worry if others in my department get their assignments done more quickly and efficiently than I do. So I often work later than I probably should, which means I spend less time with my family. I provide for my family in financial ways, but I often wonder if I'm depriving them emotionally. My brother just leaves his job at five o'clock, sometimes bringing home a pizza, and sits in front of the television watching programs his kids like but he doesn't. But he does it because he enjoys watching his children laugh. No matter what I do, I can't seem to get over the feeling that I'm never going to be as successful, happy, or contented as my brother. No matter how hard I try, I'm never going to be good enough."

What tremendous courage it took this man to be aware of his jealousy and to admit to his feeling of not being good enough! Looking so directly at the causes and conditions of suffering is an essential step in recognizing the possibility of overcoming the limitations we tend to think of as inevitable or unchangeable.

In addition to social and familial circumstances, very personal experiences can also condition people's views of themselves and their experiences. A number of people I've met and spoken with have talked about how a sleepless night, an argument with a spouse, partner, child, or colleague, or the end of a romantic relationship can adversely affect their view of themselves and the world around them.

Others, meanwhile, have entered the private interview room in whatever place I'm teaching positively glowing with happiness be-cause they've recently found their "soul mate," landed the job they've always wanted, or just closed the deal on their "dream house."

These conversations have, in many ways, deepened my own un-derstanding of the Second Noble Truth. Grasping, fixation, or thirst—however you want to define it—is, in many cases, an in-stantaneous, often unconscious response to the basic condition of impermanence: what some of my friends who work in the field of psychology might call a "defense mechanism."

Words like "attachment" and "grasping" don't really capture the complexity of the underlying nature of this mechanism, which may best be described as a kind of balancing act between hope and fear: hope that things will either change or stay the same and fear of the same things. Sometimes we're propelled in one direc-tion or another and sometimes we're caught between these two ex-tremes and don't know what to think.

One of the questions I'm asked most frequently in public teach-ings and private interviews is, "How can I get rid of attachment? How can I get rid of hope and fear?"

The simple answer is, "By not trying."

Why?

Because when we try to get rid of something, we're really just re-inforcing hope and fear. If we treat some condition, feeling, sensa-tion, or any other type of experience as an enemy, we only make it stronger: We're resisting and succumbing to it at the same time. The middle way proposed by the Buddha begins by simply *looking* at whatever it is we're thinking or feeling: *I'm angry. I'm jealous. I'm tired. I'm afraid.*

As we look, gradually we'll come to notice that thoughts and feelings aren't as fixed or solid as they originally appeared. Impermanence has its advantages. All things change—even our hopes and fears.

AN EXERCISE

Life doesn't stay in place even for a moment.

—Gampopa, *The Jewel Ornament of Liberation,*
translated by Khenpo Konchog Gyaltsen Rinpoche

Observing minute changes in our experience does take some practice. The next time you pass a bathroom mirror, stand in a way that you don't see your face. Look at the other things reflected there: the tiles on the wall, for example, or the arrangement of towels. Then look at your face. Take a moment to notice any differences in the mental and emotional responses you might experience to what you see in the mirror. Do you notice any differences in the way you respond to the "background" and your reactions to your own face?

If you can, repeat this exercise in front of the same mirror later in the day or perhaps the next day. Do you notice any changes in the background? Do you notice any changes in your own face? Chances are you'll notice some differences. The tiles may have been scrubbed or they may be a little bit more soiled. The towels or other elements of the room may be slightly rearranged. When at last you look at your face, you may notice small differences, as well.

Don't continue this exercise for very long—maybe thirty seconds or so. Just notice any sort of mental or emotional reaction to these changes: "The place looks tidier today," or "I look tired," or "I look old," or "I look fat." Whatever thoughts or emotions come up will provide insight into the particular nature of your own biases and attachments. Don't judge them or try to analyze them. Just look at them. The point of the exercise is to begin to recognize that even the simplest act of sensory perception is invariably accompanied by a veil of thoughts and emotions through which you interpret it.

If we continue looking, we'll gradually find it easier to distinguish between bare perceptions and the mental and emotional factors that accompany them. Recognizing these factors doesn't mean we have to reject or eliminate them, however. In pointing out the role of the mind in shaping our experience, the Second Noble Truth—which represents the second stage of the Buddha's diagnostic approach to the problem of suffering—prepares us for the "prognosis" of the Third.

4

THE TURNING POINT

Liberation occurs through recognizing just by that which you are bound.

> —The Ninth Gyalwa Karmapa,
> *Mahāmudrā: The Ocean of Definitive Meaning,*
> translated by Elizabeth M. Callahan

WHEN I'M TEACHING in front of large groups, I often confront a rather embarrassing problem. My throat gets dry as I talk, so I tend to drain my glass of water pretty early on in the teaching session. Invariably, people notice that my glass is empty and they very kindly refill it. As I continue to speak, my throat gets dry, I drink the entire glass of water, and sooner or later, someone refills my glass again. I go on talking or answering questions, and again someone refills my glass.

After some time—usually before the teaching period is scheduled to end—I become aware of a rather uncomfortable feeling, and a thought crosses my mind: *Oh dear, there's an hour left for this session and I have to pee.*

I talk a little bit more, answer some questions, and glance at my watch.

Now there's forty-five minutes left and I really have to pee. . . .

Half an hour passes and the urge to pee becomes intense. . . .

Someone raises his hand and asks, "What is the difference between pure awareness and conditioned awareness?"

The question goes to the heart of the Buddha's teaching about the Third Noble Truth. Often translated as "The Truth of Cessation," this third insight into the nature of experience tells us that the various forms of suffering we experience can be brought to an end.

But now I REALLY, REALLY have to pee.

So I tell him, "This is a great secret, which I'll tell you after a short break."

With all the dignity I can summon, I get up off the chair where I've been sitting, slowly pass through rows of people bowing, and finally get to a bathroom.

Now, peeing may not be anyone's idea of an enlightening experience, but I can tell you that once I empty my bladder, I recognize that the deep sense of relief I feel in that moment is a good analogy for the Third Noble Truth: that relief was with me all the time as what you might call a basic condition. I just didn't recognize it because it was temporarily obscured by all that water. But afterwards, I was able to recognize it and appreciate it.

The Buddha referred to this dilemma with a somewhat more dignified analogy in which he compared this basic nature to the sun. Though it's always shining, the sun is often obscured by clouds. Yet we can only really see the clouds because the sun is illuminating them. In the same way, our basic nature is always present. It is, in fact, what allows us to discern even those things that obscure it: an insight that may be best understood by returning to the question raised just before I left for the bathroom.

TWO TYPES OF AWARENESS

The essence of every thought that arises is pristine awareness.
—Pengar Jamphel Sangpo, *Short Invocation of Vajradhara,*
translated by Maria Montenegro

Actually there's no great secret to understanding the difference between pure awareness and conditioned awareness. They're both *awareness*, which might be roughly defined as a capacity to recognize, register, and in a sense "catalogue" every moment of experience.

Pure awareness is like a ball of clear crystal—colorless in itself but capable of reflecting anything: your face, other people, walls, furniture. If you moved it around a little, maybe you'd see different parts of the room and the size, shape, or position of the furniture might change. If you took it outside, you could see trees, birds, flowers—even the sky! What appears, though, are only reflections. They don't really exist *inside* the ball, nor do they alter its essence in any way.

Now, suppose the crystal ball were wrapped in a piece of colored silk. Everything you saw reflected in it—whether you moved it around, carried it to different rooms, or took it outside—would be shaded to some degree by the color of the silk. That's a fairly accurate description of *conditioned awareness*: a perspective colored by ignorance, desire, aversion, and the host of other obscurations born from *dzinpa*. Yet these colored reflections are simply reflections. They don't alter the nature of that which reflects them. The crystal ball is essentially colorless.

Similarly, pure awareness in itself is always clear, capable of reflecting anything, even misconceptions about itself as limited or conditioned. Just as the sun illuminates the clouds that obscure it, pure awareness enables us to experience natural suffering and the relentless drama of self-created suffering: me versus you, mine versus yours, this feeling versus that feeling, good versus bad, pleasant versus unpleasant, and so on.

The Truth of Cessation is often described as a final release from fixation, craving, or "thirst." However, while the term "cessation" seems to imply something different or better than our present experience, it is actually a matter of acknowledging the potential already inherent within us.

Cessation—or relief from *dukkha*—is possible because awareness is fundamentally clear and unconditioned. Fear, shame, guilt, greed, competiveness, and so on, are simply veils, perspectives inherited and reinforced by our cultures, our families, and personal experience. Suffering recedes, according to the Third Noble Truth, to the extent that we let go of the whole framework of grasping.

We accomplish this not by suppressing our desires, our aversions, our fixations, or trying to "think differently," but rather by turning our awareness inward, examining the thoughts, emotions, and sensations that trouble us, and beginning to notice them— and perhaps even appreciate them—as expressions of awareness itself.

Simply put, the cause of the various diseases we experience is the cure. The mind that grasps is the mind that sets us free.

BUDDHA NATURE

When you are living in darkness, why don't you look for the light?

—The Dhammapada,
translated by Eknath Easwaran

In order to explain this more clearly I have to cheat a little bit, bringing up a subject that the Buddha never explicitly mentioned in his teachings of the First Turning of The Wheel. But as a number of my teachers have admitted, this subject is implied in the first and second turnings.

It isn't as if he was holding back on some great revelation that would only be passed on to the best and brightest of his students. Rather, like a responsible teacher, he focused first of all on teaching basic principles before moving on to more advanced subjects. Ask any elementary school teacher about the practicality of teaching calculus to children who haven't yet mastered the basics of addition, subtraction, division, or multiplication.

The subject is *buddha nature*—which doesn't refer to the behavior or attitude of someone who walks around in colored robes, begging for food! *Buddha* is a Sanskrit term that might be roughly translated as "one who is awake." As a formal title, it usually refers to Siddhartha Gautama, the young man who achieved enlightenment twenty-five hundred years ago in Bodhgaya.

Buddha nature, however, is not a formal title. It's not a characteristic exclusive to the historical Buddha or to Buddhist practitioners. It's not something created or imagined. It's the heart or essence inherent in all living beings: an unlimited potential to do, see, hear, or experience anything. Because of buddha nature we can learn, we can grow, we can change. We can become buddhas in our own right.

Buddha nature can't be described in terms of relative concepts. It has to be experienced directly, and direct experience is impossible to define in words. Imagine looking at a place so vast that it surpasses our ability to describe it—the Grand Canyon, for example. You could say that it's big, that the stone walls on either side are sort of red, and that the air is dry and smells faintly like cedar. But no matter how well you describe it, your description can't really encompass the experience of being in the presence of something so vast. Or you could try describing the view from the observatory of the Taipei 101, one of the world's tallest buildings, hailed as one of the "seven wonders of the modern world." You could talk about the panorama, the way the cars and people below look like ants, or your own breathlessness at standing so high above the ground. But it still wouldn't communicate the depth and breadth of your experience.

Though buddha nature defies description, the Buddha did provide some clues in the way of signposts or maps that can help direct us toward that supremely inexpressible experience. One of the ways in which he described it was in terms of three qualities: boundless wisdom, which is the capacity to *know* anything and everything—past, present, and future; infinite capability, which consists of an unlimited power to raise ourselves and other beings from any condition of suffering; and immeasurable loving-kindness and compassion—a limitless sense of relatedness to all creatures, an open-heartedness toward others that serves as a motivation to create the conditions that enable all beings to flourish.

Undoubtedly, there are many people who fervently believe in the Buddha's description and the possibility that, through study and practice, they can realize a direct experience of unlimited wisdom, capability, and compassion. There are probably many others who think it's just a bunch of nonsense.

Oddly enough, in many of the *sutras,* the Buddha seems to have enjoyed engaging in conversation with the people who doubted what he had to say. He was, after all, only one of many teachers traveling across India in the fourth century B.C.E.—a situation similar to the one in which we find ourselves at present, in which radio, TV channels, and the Internet are flooded by teachers and teachings of various persuasions. Unlike many of his contemporaries, however, the Buddha didn't try to convince people that the method through which he found release from suffering was the only true method. A common theme running through many of the *sutras* could be summarized in modern terms as, "This is just what I did and this is what I recognized. Don't believe anything I say because I say so. Try it out for yourselves."

He didn't actively discourage people from considering what he'd learned and how he learned it. Rather, in his teachings on buddha nature, he presented his listeners with a kind of thought experiment, inviting them to discover within their own experience the ways in which aspects of buddha nature emerge from time to time in our daily lives. He presented this experiment in terms of an analogy of a house in which a lamp has been lit and the shades or shutters have been drawn. The house represents the seemingly solid perspective of physical, mental, and emotional conditioning. The lamp represents our buddha nature. No matter how tightly the shades and shutters are drawn, inevitably a bit of the light from inside the house shines through.

Inside, the light from the lamp provides the clarity to distinguish between, say, a chair, a bed, or a carpet. As it peeks through the shades or shutters we may experience the light of wisdom sometimes as intuition, what some people describe as a "gut level" feeling about a person, situation, or event.

Loving-kindness and compassion shine through the shutters in those moments when we spontaneously give aid or comfort to someone, not out of self-interest or thinking we might get something in return, but just because it seems the right thing to do. It may be something as simple as offering people a shoulder to cry on when they're in pain or helping someone cross the street, or it may involve a longer-term commitment, like sitting by the bedside of someone ill or dying. We've all heard, too, of extreme instances in which someone, without even thinking about the risk to his or her own life, jumps into a river to save a stranger who is drowning.

Capability often manifests in the way in which we survive difficult events. For example, a long-time Buddhist practitioner I met recently had invested heavily in the stock market back in the 1990s, and when the market fell later in the decade, he lost everything. Many of his friends and partners had also lost a great deal of money, and some of them went a little crazy. Some lost confidence in themselves and their ability to make decisions; some fell into deep depression; others, like the people who lost money during the stock market crash of 1929, jumped out of windows. But he didn't lose his mind or his confidence, or fall into depression. Slowly, he began investing again and built up a new, solid financial base.

Seeing his apparent calm in the face of such a terrific downturn of events, a number of his friends and associates asked him how he was able to retain his equanimity. "Well," he replied, "I got all this money from the stock market, then it went back to the stock market, and now it's coming back. Conditions change, but I'm still here. I can make decisions. So maybe I was living in a big house one year and sleeping on a friend's couch the next. That doesn't change the fact that I can choose how to think about myself and all the stuff happening around me. I consider myself very fortunate, in fact. Some people aren't capable of choosing and some people don't recognize that they *can* choose. I guess I'm lucky because I fall into the category of people who are able to recognize their capacity for choice."

I've heard similar remarks from people who are coping with chronic illness, either in themselves, their parents, their children, other family members, or friends. One man I met recently in North America, for instance, spoke at length about maintaining his job and his relationship with his wife and children while continuing to visit his father, who was suffering from Alzheimer's disease. "Of course it's hard to balance all these things," he said. "But it's what I do. I don't see any other way."

Such a simple statement, but how refreshing! Though he'd never attended a Buddhist teaching before, had never studied the literature, and didn't necessarily identify himself as Buddhist, his description of his life and the way he approached it represented a spontaneous expression of all three aspects of buddha nature: the wisdom to see the depth and breadth of his situation, the capability to choose how to interpret and act on what he saw, and the spontaneous attitude of loving-kindness and compassion.

As I listened to him, it occurred to me that these three characteristics of buddha nature can be summed up in a single word: courage—specifically the courage to *be*, just as we are, right here, right now, with all our doubts and uncertainties. Facing experience directly opens us to the possibility of recognizing that whatever we experience—love, loneliness, hate, jealousy, joy, greed, grief, and so on—is, in essence, an expression of the fundamentally unlimited potential of our buddha nature.

This principle is implied in the "positive prognosis" of the Third Noble Truth. Whatever discomfort we feel—subtle, intense, or somewhere in between—subsides to the degree that we cut through our fixation upon a very limited, conditioned, and conditional view of ourselves and begin to identify with the capability to experience anything at all. Eventually, it's possible to come to rest in buddha nature itself—the way, for instance, a bird might rest in coming home to its nest.

In that moment, suffering ends. There is nothing to fear, nothing to resist. Not even death can trouble you.

This point was driven home very clearly to me as I sat with my father during the final days and hours of his life. I was twenty-one years old at the time, and my father was seventy-six. He was a great meditator who had spent his entire life deepening his recognition of the immensity of the mind and the transience of perception as he'd been taught, and passing his understanding along to thousands of students from around the world. Scores of people came to visit him during the final days of his life: monks, nuns, family members, other teachers, former students, and ordinary people from surrounding villages. Sometimes he would sit up to meet them and at other times he would have to lie down. To every visitor he offered a gentle smile and a softly murmured "thank you." There was no trace of fear in his features, no evidence of struggle in his thin frame. The only sign that he was undergoing an extraordinary transition was the expression of mild curiosity that sometimes crossed his face, and of course, the quiet finality with which he thanked each and every visitor, as if to say that they had been his teachers rather than the other way around.

In the final few moments of his life, he felt an urge to urinate. Because the bathroom was far down the hall, there was a portable sort of toilet in his room, and as someone brought it toward him, he began to stand up from his bed.

"Maybe you'd better just stay lying down," one of my brothers suggested. "We can put this thing under you."

"No, no," he laughed, waving our concerns aside.

When he'd finished, he sat back on his bed in meditation posture—legs crossed, spine straight, hands resting comfortably in his lap, and eyes focused straight ahead. Very gradually, his breathing slowed and finally stopped. We didn't even realize that he'd died for several moments. He remained in that meditative posture, which in Tibetan is known as *tuk dam* (which could very roughly be understood as "death meditation"—a process of consciously experiencing the separation of consciousness from the physical body) for three days before his body began to slump. During that period, his body wasn't stiff with *rigor mortis*, and his complexion remained bright pink, and even slightly radiant. I can well understand that these are conditions that many people in the modern world would find difficult to believe. I'd find them hard to believe if I hadn't witnessed them myself—and I was raised in a tradition in which it is considered possible that a person can experience death with full consciousness and equanimity. But the signs were there. My father died with full awareness, looking calmly at what most people consider the most dire form of suffering as a luminous expression of his buddha nature.

BUDDHA MOMENTS

Every sentient being has the potential to improve and become enlightened.

—The Twelfth Tai Situpa, *Awakening the Sleeping Buddha*,
edited by Lea Terhune

Most of us don't recognize our buddha nature until it's pointed out to us.

Not long ago, I heard a story about a man in India who was given an expensive watch. Having no experience of what a watch is or does, he thought of it as nothing more than a pretty bracelet. He had no idea that it was an instrument that told time. Consequently, he was always late for work, was ultimately fired from his job, and lost his home. Although he made appointments with various prospective employers, he was either too late or too early for the interview. Finally, out of frustration, he asked a man on the street, "Can you tell me what time it is?"

The man looked at him in surprise.

"You're wearing a watch," he said. "That will tell you what time it is."

"A watch?" the fellow replied. "What's that?"

"You're kidding, right?" the stranger said, pointing to the instrument the guy was wearing on his wrist.

"No," the man answered. "This thing is a nice piece of jewelry. It was given to me by a friend. What does it have to do with knowing what time it is?"

So, exhibiting a good deal of patience, the stranger on the street taught him to read the hour and minute hands on his watch, and even the swiftly moving hand that swept over seconds.

"I can't believe this!" the fellow exclaimed. "Do you mean to say that I've always had something that would tell me the time and I never even knew it?"

"Don't blame me," the stranger said. "Whoever gave it to you should have explained what it is."

After a moment, the man replied in a quiet, embarrassed voice, "Well, maybe he didn't know what it was, either."

"Be that as it may," the stranger replied, "he gave you a gift that you didn't know how to use. Now, at least, you know how to use it."

And with that he disappeared into the swirl of pedestrians, beggars, cars, and rickshaws that crowd the busy streets of India.

Who knows whether this fellow was a buddha or just a random stranger encountered by chance, who happened to know the difference between a watch and a bracelet. In any case, the man was able to make use of his watch, show up on time for interviews, eventually get a good job, and reestablish his life. The lesson I learned from this story is that we're endowed with capacities that we frequently fail to recognize until they're pointed out to us. These reminders are what I like to call "buddha moments"— opportunities to wake up, so to speak, from the dream of conditioned awareness.

I experienced one such buddha moment during my first teaching tour in California, when people urged me to swim as a form of exercise. I didn't want to go, but my hosts had already set up an appointment at a local club, which was outfitted with an Olympic-sized pool. I jumped in and was immediately a success—at swimming underwater: which is to say, I sank like a stone. I kept trying to push myself along underwater, but I couldn't last for more than a minute. My arms and legs got tired and I couldn't hold my breath. "Okay," I figured, "you're being too tense, trying to accomplish something." So I let my muscles relax completely, floated up to the surface, and again was successful—at sinking.

Then I remembered something: As a child I used to swim in a small pond near my home. It was not a very deep pond, and my swimming style wasn't exactly what you'd call elegant—just flapping along dog paddling.

The people who'd brought me to the club were amazed. "One minute you were sinking," they said, "and the next minute you were swimming. How did you do that?"

"I remembered," I answered. "For a few moments I was confused by the size of the pool. Then I remembered that I could swim."

This experience is similar—perhaps on a small scale—to the recollection of the power and potential of buddha nature. Deep within us lies the capacity for boundless wisdom, capability, and compassion. We tend not to remember our ability until we're thrust into sink-or-swim situations.

SEEING THE GOOD

I rejoice with delight at the good done by all beings.
—Śāntideva, *The Bodhicaryāvatāra*,
translated by Kate Crosby and Andre Skilton

In talking with many psychologists during my travels I learned of an interesting quirk of human nature: If we have ten qualities— nine of them positive and one of them negative—most people will tend to focus almost exclusively on the one negative quality and forget about the positive ones.

I saw this for myself not long ago when I received a late-night phone call from a friend of mine who is a rather popular performer. She was in Europe at the time and had just returned to her hotel room after appearing before thousands of enthusiastic fans. Imagine appearing in front of that many people and hearing them shout how much they love you and how wonderful you are!

After the concert, she returned to her hotel room to work on her laptop. Unfortunately, the battery was dead and she didn't have the proper adapter to plug in and recharge her computer. She called the front desk for assistance and they promised to come up right away. Minutes passed, no one showed up, and she started to get rather upset. All sorts of feelings emerged: anger, resentment, and loneliness over not being able to connect with the outside world through e-mail or the Internet.

Finally, she called me—I was teaching in Paris at the time—and asked, "What can I do? Just appearing on a sidewalk makes thousands of people happy, but alone in my hotel room I'm miserable. This stupid little problem with the computer has ruined my night."

We talked for a bit about accepting impermanence and the challenges of fixating on relative reality. I remember telling her, "You tried your best to do something about your computer, but if the problem isn't solved as quickly as you want it to be, you can use the frustration and anger you feel as a focus of meditation. Don't run from those feelings. Don't try to shove them away. Look at them directly. If you do that, you might be able to see the awareness that enables you to be conscious of these feelings. If you can even touch that awareness, you'll start to see the problem you're experiencing now in the context of all the good qualities you have:

your talent, for example, and the capability of giving joy to thousands of people. There is so much good in you and so much that is good about your life. Why let one difficult situation blind you to all the positive things you bring to the world?"

We talked a bit longer until she calmed down and realized that one unfortunate incident didn't really have to ruin her night, and it didn't undermine her capacity to bring joy to other people.

"I feel better just talking to you," she said. "Thanks for reminding me that one little problem won't ruin my life."

After I hung up the phone, I thought a bit about our conversation. Moments later, I realized what I had wanted to say, but hadn't had the time to formulate as a complete idea. Wisdom, capability, loving-kindness, and compassion are what we're born with. Frustration, jealousy, guilt, shame, anxiety, greed, competitiveness, and so on, are experiences we learn, often through the influences of our culture, our families, and our friends, and reinforced by personal experience.

The "positive prognosis" of the Third Noble Truth is that the limited or limiting ideas we hold about ourselves, others, and every other experience can be unlearned.

STONES

Oneself is one's own refuge; what other refuge can there be?
—The Dhammapada,
translated by Ven. Dr. Rewata Dhamma

In order to offer people of various temperaments and backgrounds the opportunity to taste the immense possibilities of their buddha nature, the Buddha taught a number of different practices. One of these involves taking a kind of "inventory" of our qualities and characteristics. In the Tibetan tradition we conduct this inventory by making piles of colored stones. Black stones represent our negative qualities and white stones represent our positive qualities.

At first, perhaps, the pile of black stones may be bigger than the pile of white ones. But then we take a moment to consider, "Well, I said something really nice to someone today, which made that person smile." So we add a white stone to our pile. "I said or did something nice to someone I don't like or with whom I've some difficulties." Exercising loving-kindness and compassion is certainly worth a couple of white stones. "I have a mind capable of making choices." That's worth at least a few more white stones. "I'm using this mind to recognize its capacity to make choices." Add at least another five white stones to the pile. "I *want* to use my mind to recognize the capability of my mind to make choices." Ten white stones, at least. "My mind is free to choose a means of experiencing peace and happiness that offers others the same experience of peace and happiness." A landslide of white stones!

You don't have to use stones to carry out this exercise; they're just easy to find in rural parts of Tibet. You can use slips of paper, coins, shells, or whatever comes in handy. You can even use a sheet of paper to make a list of your qualities and characteristics. The point of the inventory is to enable yourself to recognize your positive characteristics, which you exercise sometimes without even thinking.

This type of personal examination is a simple and quite effective means of connecting with your essential nature. It's especially useful during those times when under the sway of a strong emotion: anger, jealousy, loneliness, or fear. In fact, if we begin "counting stones" during moments of strong emotion or while facing a difficult situation, then that emotion or situation in itself becomes a powerful incentive to actively practice recognizing our boundless capacities.

The circumstances and conditions that define material life are always relative, always changing. Today we might feel healthy and whole; tomorrow we may have the flu. Today we might be getting along with everybody; tomorrow we might have an argument. At this moment, we may enjoy the leisure and opportunity to read a book; a moment from now, we may find ourselves in the midst of dealing with some sort of personal or professional difficulty.

With practice, any experience can become an opportunity to discover our essential wisdom, capability, loving-kindness, and compassion. Doing so, however, involves cutting through certain entrenched beliefs and attitudes—"the treatment plan" the Buddha prescribed for the relief from suffering. This plan is laid out in the Fourth Noble Truth, often referred to as the "Truth of the Path."

5

BREAKING THROUGH

If the doors of perception were cleansed, everything
would appear as it is . . .
—WILLIAM BLAKE, "The Marriage of Heaven and Hell"

IN THEIR WRITINGS and their teachings, Buddhist masters observe that all creatures want to attain happiness and avoid suffering. Of course, this observation is not confined to Buddhist teachings or to any particular philosophical, psychological, scientific, or spiritual discipline. It's a commonsense deduction based on looking at the way we and the other creatures with whom we share this world behave.

By now it should be clear that there are many varieties and degrees of suffering, all of which can be categorized as *dukkha*. But what is happiness? How can we define it? How can we attain it? Is there any one thing that everyone can agree on that makes us happy?

This last is a question I often ask when I teach, and the answers always vary. Some people say "Money." Some people say "Love." Some people say "Peace." Some people say "Gold." Once I even heard someone say "Chilies!"

What I find most interesting is that for every answer there's an opposite response. Some people don't want riches; they prefer to live simply. Some people prefer to live alone. Some people like to argue and fight for what they believe is right. And of course, some people don't like chilies.

After the answers stop coming, silence settles on the room, as everybody present realizes that there is no single thing that everyone can agree on. Gradually, it begins to dawn on the people gathered in the room that the answers given represent either objects that exist outside or beyond themselves or conditions that are in some way other than what they experience right here, right now. At this point, the silence grows deeper and more contemplative as one by one, people begin to recognize that a simple question-and-answer exercise, conducted in a spirit of fun and often accompanied by laughter, has exposed deeply ingrained habits of perception and belief that are almost guaranteed to perpetuate suffering and inhibit the possibility of discovering an enduring, unconditional state of happiness.

Among these habits is the tendency to define our experience in dualistic terms: "self" and "other"; "mine" and "not mine"; and "pleasant" and "unpleasant." In itself, relating to the world dualistically isn't any great tragedy. In fact, as discussed earlier, we're biologically disposed and conditioned by our cultural, familial, and individual backgrounds to make distinctions—not only for their survival value but also for the role they play in social interaction and the performance of daily tasks. From a simply practical point of view, the ability to "map" and navigate our daily lives in dualistic terms is essential.

In talking to people over the years, however, I've encountered a common misconception that Buddhism considers dualistic perception as a kind of defect. That is not the case. Neither the Buddha nor any of the great masters who followed in his footsteps have said that there is something inherently wrong or harmful in relating to the world in dualistic terms. Rather, they explain, defining experience in terms of "subject" and "object," "self" and "other," and so on, is simply one aspect of awareness: a useful, if limited, tool.

To use a very simple analogy, we can accomplish many tasks with our hands: typing, chopping vegetables, dialing telephone numbers, scrolling through the list of songs on an MP3 player, opening and closing doors, and buttoning shirts or blouses. You can probably add a long list of useful ways to use your hands. But would you be willing to say that whatever you can do with your hands represents your entire range of capabilities? Yes, if you work at it, you can probably walk on your hands. But can you see with them, hear with them, or smell with them? Can your hands digest food, maintain the functions of your heart or liver, or make decisions? Unless you've been gifted with unusual powers, the answer to these questions will be "no," and you'd dismiss the idea that whatever your hands do represents the entire range of your capabilities.

While we can easily admit that our hands don't represent our entire range of abilities, it's a bit more difficult to recognize that splitting experience into opposing terms such as "subject" and "object," "self" and "other," or "mine" and "not mine" represents only a fraction of the capacity of our buddha nature. Until we're introduced to the possibility of a different way of relating to experience, and embrace the possibility of exploring it, our dualistic perspective and the variety of mental and emotional habits that arise from it prevent us from experiencing the full range of our inherent potential.

DELUSION AND ILLUSION

Self-deception is a constant problem.

—Chögyam Trungpa, *Cutting Through Spiritual Materialism,*
    edited by John Baker and Marvin Casper

Imagine putting on a pair of dark green sunglasses. Everything you see would appear in shades of green: green people, green cars, green buildings, green rice, and green pizza. Even your own hands and feet would look green. If you took off your sunglasses, your entire experience would change. "Oh, people aren't green!" "My hands aren't green!" "My face isn't green!" "Pizza isn't green!"

But what if you never took off your sunglasses? What if you believed that you couldn't get through life without them, that you'd become so attached to wearing them that you'd never even consider taking them off, even when you went to bed? Certainly, you could get through life seeing everything in shades of green. But you'd miss out on seeing so many different colors. And once you became accustomed to seeing things in shades of green, you'd rarely pause to consider that green may not be the only color you could see. You'd begin to believe wholeheartedly that everything is green.

Similarly, certain mental and emotional habits condition our worldview. We become attached to a "sunglass point of view." We believe that the way we see things is the way they truly are.

Our biology, culture, and personal experiences work together to mistake relative distinctions as absolute truths and concepts as direct experiences. This fundamental discrepancy almost invariably fosters a haunting sense of unease, a kind of "free-floating" *dukkha* lurking in the background of awareness as a nagging sense of incompleteness, isolation, or instability.

In an effort to combat this basic unease, we tend to invest the "inhabitants" of our relative or conditional world—ourselves, other people, objects, and situations—with qualities that enhance their semblance of solidness and stability. But this strategy clouds our perspective even further. In addition to mistaking relative distinctions as absolute, we bury this mistaken view in layers of illusion.

THE FIRST STEP

Suffering has good qualities.

—*Engaging in the Conduct of Bodhisattvas,*
translated by Khenpo Konchag Gyaltsen Rinpoche

The Fourth Noble Truth, the Truth of the Path, teaches us that in order to bring an end to suffering we need to cut through dualistic habits of perception and the illusions that hold them in place—not by fighting or suppressing them, but by embracing and exploring them. *Dukkha,* however it manifests, is our guide along a path that ultimately leads to discovering the source from which it springs. By facing it directly, we begin to use it, rather than be used by it.

At first, we might not see much more than a blur of thoughts, feelings, and sensations that all run together so fast and furiously that it's impossible to distinguish one from another. But with a bit of patient effort, we'll begin to make out an entire landscape of ideas, attitudes, and beliefs—most of which initially appear quite solid, sensible, and firmly rooted in reality. *Yes*, we might think, *that's the way things are.*

Yet as we continue to look, we start to notice a few cracks and holes. Maybe our ideas aren't as solid as we imagined. The longer we look at them, the more cracks we see, until eventually the whole set of beliefs and opinions on which we've based our understanding of ourselves and the world around us begins to crumble. Understandably, we may experience some confusion or disorientation as this happens. However, once the dust begins to settle, we find ourselves face-to-face with a much more direct and profound understanding of our own nature and the nature of reality.

Before setting out on the path, though, we might find it useful to familiarize ourselves with the terrain; not only to develop some idea of where we're going, but also to alert ourselves to "bumps"—fixed beliefs that are especially hard to penetrate—we're likely to hit along the way. As a young student at Sherab Ling, I was taught to look out for three such "bumps" in particular: permanence, singularity, and independence.

PERMANENCE

> *Think that nothing lasts.*
>
> —Jamgon Kongtrul, *The Torch of Certainty*,
>   translated by Judith Hanson

Cars and computers break down. People move away, change jobs, grow up, grow old, get sick, and eventually die. As we look at our experience, we can recognize that we're no longer infants or schoolchildren. We can see, and often welcome, other major transitions, like graduating from college, getting married, having children, and moving to a new home or a new job. Sometimes the changes we undergo aren't so pleasant. Like other people, we get sick, we grow old, and eventually we die. Maybe we lose our jobs or the person we're married to or romantically involved with announces "I don't love you anymore."

Yet even as we acknowledge certain changes, on a very subtle level we cling to the idea of *permanence*: a belief that an essential core of "me," "others," and so on, remains constant throughout time. The "me" I was yesterday is the same "me" I am today. The table or book we saw yesterday is the same table or book we see today. The Mingyur Rinpoche who gave a talk yesterday is the same Mingyur Rinpoche giving a talk today. Even our emotions sometimes seem permanent: "I was angry at my boss yesterday, I'm angry at him today, and I'll be angry at him tomorrow. I'll never forgive him!"

The Buddha compared this delusion to climbing a tree that looks strong and whole on the outside but is hollow and rotten on the inside. The higher we climb, the more tightly we cling to the lifeless branches, and the more likely it is that one of those branches will break. Eventually, we must fall—and the pain of that fall will be greater the higher we climb.

On a mental and emotional level, for example, "you," "me," and other people are always changing. I can't say that the "me" I was at nine years old is the same "me" I was at nineteen, or even at thirty. The nine-year-old "me" was a child full of anxiety, frightened by loud noises, and terrified of being a failure in his father's eyes and in the eyes of his father's students. The nineteen-year-old "me" had graduated from two three-year retreat programs aimed at mastering the deeper practices of Tibetan Buddhist meditation, attending one monastic school while helping to build another, running the day-to-day functions of a large monastery in India, and teaching monks who were much older than he was. The thirty-three-year-old "me" spends a good deal of time in airports, traveling between many different countries, facing hundreds of people at a time in an attempt to deliver teachings and instructions at several different levels of sophistication; meeting in private with individuals or small groups of people who seek deeper insight into their personal practice; making international phone calls to plan a teaching tour for a year ahead; and learning bits and pieces of several different languages in order to make a connection with the people around the world. He also advises people from a wide variety of backgrounds in dealing with personal problems including chronic pain, depression, divorce, emotional and physical abuse, and the physical and emotional toll involved in caring for friends and family members who are ill or dying.

Similarly, "others" undergo mental and emotional changes. I've spoken to a number of people who are mystified by the fact that they can be talking one day to someone they know and everything seems fine. The other person is happy, looking forward to life, and ready to meet the challenges of the day. A day or maybe a week later, that same person is angry or depressed; he or she can't get out of bed or just can't see any hope in his or her life. Sometimes the changes are so dramatic—for example, as a result of alcoholism or some other addiction—we might find ourselves thinking, "I don't even recognize this person anymore!"

In addition, as I've learned through conversations with scientists over the years, our physical bodies are undergoing constant change on levels far below conscious awareness or control—producing hormones, for example, or regulating body temperature. By the time you've finished reading this sentence, some of the cells in your body have already have been eliminated and replaced by new ones. The molecules, atoms, and subatomic particles that make up those cells have shifted.

Even the molecules, atoms, and subatomic particles that make up this book—as well as the furniture in the room where you're reading it—are always shifting and changing, moving around. The pages of the book may start to yellow or wrinkle. Cracks may appear in the wall of your room. A bit of paint might chip off a nearby table.

Taking all these things into consideration, where can one find permanence?

SINGULARITY

> *Each moment is similar and because of the similarity, we are deluded.*
>
> —Gampopa, *The Jewel Ornament of Liberation*,
> translated by Khenpo Kongchog Gyaltsen Rinpoche

From the delusion of permanence arises the idea of *singularity*—the belief that the "essential core" that persists through time is indivisible and uniquely identifiable. Even when we say things like "That experience changed me" or "I look at the world differently now," we're still affirming a sense of "me" as a single whole, an inner "face" through which we gaze at the world.

Singularity is such a subtle delusion that it's hard to see until it's pointed out to us. For example, a woman recently confided, "I'm stuck in an impossible marriage. I loved my husband when I married him, but now I hate him. I have three children, though, and I don't want to put them through a long divorce battle. I want them to have a positive relationship with their father. I don't want to move them from the house they've grown up in, but I don't want to rely on financial support from my husband."

What's the word most frequently repeated in this series of statements?

"I."

But who is "I"? Is "I" the person who loved her husband but now hates him? Is "I" the mother of three children who wants to avoid a long divorce battle or the woman who wants her children to develop a positive relationship with their father? How many "I's" are there? One? Two? Three?

The likely response is that there's only one "I," who reacts in different ways to different situations, who expresses different aspects of herself in relation to other people, or who—in response to new ideas and experiences, or changes in circumstances and conditions—has developed a different set of attitudes and feelings.

Given all these differences, can "I" really be one?

Similarly, we might ask ourselves if the "I" that responds in certain ways to a particular situation—an argument with a coworker or family member, perhaps—is the same "I" that responds in other ways to other situations, like reading a book, watching television, or checking e-mail.

Our tendency is to say, "Well, they're all parts of me."

But if there are "parts," can there be one?

INDEPENDENCE

Does the self exist within a name?

—Gampopa, *The Jewel Ornament of Liberation*,
  translated by Khenpo Kongchog Gyaltsen Rinpoche

Sometimes when I'm teaching, I ask people to play a sort of game, hiding most of my body behind my outer robe and just leaving my thumb sticking out. "Is this Mingyur Rinpoche?" I ask.

"No," most people will reply.

So then I'll stick out my whole hand and ask, "How about this? Is this Mingyur Rinpoche?"

Again, most people will say "No."

If I stick out my arm and ask the same question, most people will also answer "No."

But if I let my outer robe fall back into place so people can see my face, my arms, and so on, and ask the same question, the answer isn't always so clear. "Well, now that we can see all of you, that's Mingyur Rinpoche," some people might say.

But this "all" is made of many different parts: thumbs, hands, arms, head, legs, heart, lungs, etc. And these parts are made up of smaller parts: skin, bone, blood vessels, and the cells that make them up; the atoms that make up the cells; and the particles that make up the atoms. Certain other factors, for example, the culture in which I was raised, the training I received, my experiences in retreat, and the conversations I've had with people around the world over the past twelve years could also be considered "parts" of "Mingyur Rinpoche."

The place where someone is sitting in a public lecture room may also condition the way "Mingyur Rinpoche" appears. People sitting to the left or right may only see one side of him; people sitting directly in front may see his whole body; and people sitting in the back of the room may see a kind of a blurry image. Likewise, someone walking down the street may see "Mingyur Rinpoche" as "another of those smiling bald guys in red robes." People who may be attending their first Buddhist teaching might see "Mingyur Rinpoche" as "a smiling bald guy in red robes who has some interesting ideas and a couple of good jokes." Long-term students may see "Mingyur Rinpoche" as a reincarnated lama, spiritual guide, and personal advisor.

So while "Mingyur Rinpoche" may appear as an independent person, this appearance is made up of a lot of different parts and conditioned by a variety of circumstances. Like permanence and singularity, independence is a relative concept: a way of defining ourselves, other people, places, objects—even thoughts and emotions—as self-existing, self-contained "things-in-themselves."

But we can see from our own experience that independence is an illusion. Would we say, for example, that we are our thumb? Our arm? Our hair? Are we the pain we might feel somewhere right now in our bodies, the illness we might be experiencing? Are we the person someone else sees walking down the street or sitting across from us at the dinner table?

Likewise, if we examine people, places, and objects around us, we can recognize that none of them are inherently independent, but made up of a number of different, interrelated parts, causes, and conditions. A chair, for instance, has to at least have legs and a kind of base on which to sit, a back we can lean against. Take away the legs or the seat or the back and it wouldn't be a chair, but a few pieces of wood or metal or whatever material the parts are made of. And this material, like parts of our bodies, is made up of molecules, atoms, subatomic particles that make up the atoms, and ultimately—from the perspective of modern physicists— packets of energy that make up subatomic particles.

All of these smaller parts, moreover, had to come together under the right circumstances to form the basic material that would be used to construct a chair. In addition, somebody—or more likely, more than one person—had to be involved in creating the different parts of the chair. Somebody had to cut down a tree for wood, for example, or gather the raw materials to create glass or metal, the fabric that covers the chair, and the stuffing that goes inside the fabric. Someone else had to shape all these materials and still others had to be involved in putting the parts together, assigning a price, shipping the completed chair to a store, and putting it on display. Then somebody had to buy it and move it to a home or office.

So even a simple object like a chair isn't an inherently existing "thing-in-itself," but rather emerges from a combination of causes and conditions—a principle known in Buddhist terms as *interdependence*. Even thoughts, feelings, and sensations aren't things-in-themselves, but occur through a variety of causes and conditions. Anger or frustration might be traced back to a sleepless night, an argument, or pressure to meet a deadline. I've met a number of people who were physically or emotionally abused by their parents or other adults. "I'm a loser," they'll sometimes say. "I'll never be able to find a good job or a lasting relationship." "I wake up in a cold sweat some nights, and some days, when I see my manager approaching, my heart beats so hard I think it may punch right through my chest."

Yet just as impermanence has its advantages—inviting the possibility of changing jobs, for example, or recovering from an illness—interdependence can also work in our favor. One Canadian student of mine, acting on the advice of a friend, began attending a support group for adults who had been abused in one way or another as children. Over several months of discussing her own experiences and listening to other people describe theirs, the shame and insecurity that had haunted her for much of her life began to waver and then to lift. "For years, it was like listening to the same song over and over," she later explained. "Now I can hear the whole CD."

She hadn't studied Buddhism at all during this period. But with the help of her new friends, she'd uncovered an insight central to the Buddha's teachings.

EMPTINESS

> *There is nothing that can be described as either existing or*
> *not existing.*
>
> —The Third Karmapa,
> *Mahāmudrā: Boundless Joy and Freedom,*
> translated by Maria Montenegro

During public teachings and private interviews, someone inevitably asks a big question. Though the words and phrasing vary from person to person, the essence is the same. "If everything is relative, impermanent, and interdependent, if nothing can be said to be definitely one thing or another, does that mean I'm not real? You're not real? My feelings aren't real? This room isn't real?"

There are four possible answers, simultaneously arising, equally true and false.

Yes.

No.

Yes and no.

Neither yes nor no.

Are you confused? Great! Confusion is a big breakthrough: a sign of cutting through attachment to a particular point of view and stepping into a broader dimension of experience.

Although the boxes in which we organize our experience—like "me," "mine," "self," "other," "subject," "object," "pleasant," and "painful"—are inventions of the mind, we still experience "me-ness," "other-ness," "pain," "pleasure," and so on. We see chairs, tables, cars, and computers. We feel the joys and pangs of change. We get angry; we get sad. We seek happiness in people, places, and things, and try our best to shield ourselves from situations that cause us pain.

It would be absurd to deny these experiences. At the same time, if we begin to examine them closely, we can't point to anything and say "Yes! That's definitely permanent! That's singular! That's independent!"

If we continue breaking down our experiences into smaller and smaller pieces, investigating their relationships, looking for the causes and conditions that underlie other causes and conditions, eventually we hit what some people might call a "dead end."

It's not an end, though, and certainly not dead.

It's our first glimpse of *emptiness*, the ground from which all experience emerges.

Emptiness, the main subject of the Second Turning of the Wheel of Dharma, is probably one of the most confusing terms in Buddhist philosophy. Even long-term students of Buddhism have a hard time understanding it. Maybe that's why the Buddha waited sixteen years after turning the First Wheel of Dharma to start talking about it.

Actually, it's pretty simple, once you get past your initial preconceptions about the meaning.

Emptiness is a rough translation of the Sanskrit term *śūnyatā* and the Tibetan term *tongpa-nyi*. The Sanskrit word *śūnya* means "zero." The Tibetan word *tongpa* means "empty"; nothing there. The Sanskrit syllable *ta* and the Tibetan syllable *nyi* don't mean anything in themselves. But when added to an adjective or noun, they convey a sense of possibility or open-endedness. So when Buddhists talk about emptiness, we don't mean "zero," but a "zero-ness": not a thing in itself, but rather a background, an infinitely open "space" that allows for anything to appear, change, disappear, and reappear.

That's very good news.

If everything were permanent, singular, or independent, nothing would change. We'd be stuck forever as we are. We couldn't grow and we couldn't learn. No one and nothing could affect us. There would be no relation between cause and effect. We could press a light switch and nothing would happen. We could dip a bag of tea into a cup of hot water a million times, but the water wouldn't affect the tea and the tea wouldn't affect the water.

But that isn't the case, is it? If we press a button on a lamp, for example, the bulb lights up. If we dip a tea bag in a cup of hot water for a few moments, we end up with a delightful cup of tea. So to return to the questions regarding whether we are real, whether our thoughts and feelings are real, and whether the room in which we presently reside is real, we can answer "yes" in the sense that we experience these phenomena and "no" in the sense that if we look beyond these experiences, we can't find anything that can be identified as inherently existing. Thoughts, feelings, chairs, chili peppers, the people in line at a grocery store—even the grocery store itself—can only be defined in comparison to something or someone else. They appear in our experience through the combination of many different causes and conditions. They are always in flux, constantly changing as they "collide" with other causes and conditions, which collide with other causes and conditions, on and on and on.

So on one hand we can't really say that anything we experience inherently exists. That's one way to look at emptiness. On the other hand, we can say that, since all of our experience emerges through the temporary collision of causes and conditions, there is nothing that is *not* emptiness.

In other words, the basic nature, or *absolute reality*, of all experience is emptiness. "Absolute," however, does not imply something solid or permanent. Emptiness is, itself, "empty" of any definable characteristics: not zero, but not nothing. You could say that emptiness is an open-ended potential for any and all sorts of experience to appear or disappear—the way a crystal ball is capable of reflecting all sorts of colors because it is, in itself, free from any color.

Now, what does that imply about the "experiencer"?

BEING AND SEEING

To be absolutely nothing is to be everything.

—James W. Douglas, *Resistance and Contemplation:
The Way of Liberation*

We wouldn't be able to experience all the wonders and terrors of phenomena if we didn't have the capacity to perceive them. All the thoughts, feelings, and other events we meet in daily life stem from a fundamental capacity to experience anything whatsoever. The qualities of buddha nature such as wisdom, capability, loving-kindness, and compassion have been described by the Buddha and the masters who followed him as "boundless," "limitless," and "infinite." They are beyond conception but charged with possibility. In other words, the very basis of buddha nature is emptiness.

But it isn't a zombie-like emptiness. *Clarity*, or what we might call a fundamental awareness that allows us to recognize and distinguish among phenomena, is also a basic characteristic of buddha nature, inseparable from emptiness. As thoughts, feelings, sensations, and so on, emerge, we become aware of them. The experience and the experiencer are one and the same. "Me" and the experience of "me" occur simultaneously, as do "other" and awareness of "other," or "car" and the awareness of "car."

Some psychologists refer to this as an "innocent perspective," a raw awareness unchained by expectations or judgments, which can emerge spontaneously in the first few moments of visiting some huge place, like Yosemite National Park, the Himalayas, or the Potala Palace in Tibet. The panorama is so vast, you don't distinguish between "I" and "what I see." There's just seeing.

It's commonly misunderstood, however, that in order to attain this innocent perspective, we somehow have to eliminate, suppress, or disengage from relative perception, and the hopes, fears, and other factors that support it. This is something of a misinterpretation of the Buddha's teachings. Relative perception is an expression of buddha nature, just as relative reality is an expression of absolute reality. Our thoughts, emotions, and sensations are like waves rising and falling in an endless ocean of infinite possibility. The problem is that we've become used to seeing only the waves and mistaking them for the ocean. Each time we look at the waves, though, we become a little more aware of the ocean; and as that happens, our focus begins to shift. We begin to identify with the ocean rather than the waves, watching them rise and fall without affecting the nature of the ocean itself.

But that can only happen if we begin to look.

MOVING FORWARD

Exert yourself again and again in cutting through.
—The Ninth Gyalwa Karmapa,
Mahāmudrā: The Ocean of Definitive Meaning,
translated by Elizabeth M. Callahan

The Buddha was very skillful in presenting his "treatment plan" for *dukkha*. Though he never explicitly discussed emptiness or buddha nature in his teachings on the Four Noble Truths, he understood that cultivating an understanding of the basic issue of suffering and its causes—sometimes interpreted as *relative wisdom*—would eventually lead us to *absolute wisdom*: a profound insight into the basis, not only of experience, but also of the experiencer.

Relative wisdom, acknowledging limited and limiting beliefs and behaviors, is only part of the path of cessation: what you might call the "preparation stage." In order to actually cut through our self-imposed limitations, we need to spend a little time observing our mental and emotional habits, befriending them, and perhaps discovering within our most challenging experiences a powerful company of bodyguards.

The exercises in the previous chapters offered a taste of the benefits we can experience through examining our thoughts, feelings, and situations. Part Two takes the process deeper, presenting in detail three transformative "tools" through which we can embrace the challenges and changes in our lives, and discover the seeds of courage, wisdom, and joy that lie within us, waiting to blossom.

PART TWO

EXPERIENCE

*It is to guide students well that
I taught different approaches.*

—*Laṅkāvatārasūtra,*
  translated by Maria Montenegro

6

TOOLS OF TRANSFORMATION

We are in a situation of someone who possesses a
beautiful car but doesn't know how to drive.
—Bokar Rinpoche, *Meditation: Advice to Beginners,*
translated by Christiane Buchet

THERE'S AN OLD Buddhist saying: "In order to fly, a bird needs
two wings." One of those "wings" is an understanding of the principles of suffering, buddha nature, emptiness, and so on—
referred to earlier as relative wisdom, recognizing the way things
are through analyzing experience. But relative wisdom on its own
is only the beginning of the path of transformation. It needs to be
applied in order to be made a part of one's own life.

Application, also known as "method," is the other wing of the
bird: the means, or process, through which relative wisdom is
transformed into an actual experience of freedom that is beyond
subject and object, self and other, or positive and negative.

The importance of combining wisdom and method can be made
a little bit clearer through the story of Ananda, the Buddha's
cousin who became his closest personal attendant. Ananda did his
best to ensure that the Buddha was comfortable, helping to make

sure that wherever he was traveling, he had food, a nice place to sleep, and protection from the elements of heat, wind, cold, and rain. Ananda also had quite a good memory and was able to recite the Buddha's teachings word for word. "If you give any teaching," he asked his cousin, "I want to hear it." Of course, the Buddha agreed.

There was only one slight problem: Ananda could repeat the Buddha's teachings but he didn't spend much time practicing them.

But another fellow, Mahākāśyapa, not only listened, but also put what he'd learned into practice and attained the same state of freedom and clarity as the Buddha had. As the Buddha lay dying, he appointed Mahākāśyapa as his main lineage holder—that is to say, the person who could pass on to others not only the *teachings* but the actual *experience* of freedom.

"After you," he added. "Ananda can be my main lineage holder."

Mahākāśyapa, of course, accepted, yet he pondered: "How can I help Ananda, since he so rarely practices?"

As he considered the problem, he came up with a rather ingenious plan. After the Buddha died, Mahākāśyapa—to put it in modern terms—"fired" Ananda. "Please leave this area," he said, "because when Buddha was alive you didn't treat him with proper respect and you made a lot of mistakes."

Ananda, of course, was very upset. "When Buddha was alive," he thought, "I was most important—now Mahākāśyapa fires me!"

He went away to another district of India where there were many people who had heard the Buddha and wanted further teachings. So Ananda taught, and his students put the teachings into practice. Many achieved the freedom of mind—the direct, clear awareness of experience that doesn't change the nature of the experiencer—which the Buddha had achieved. But Ananda still didn't put much effort into practice.

As the story goes, during meditation one of his students saw into Ananda's mind and realized that he had not yet attained enlightenment. The student said to him, "Please, teacher, meditate! You aren't free."

Now Ananda was really distraught. "Even my students have gone beyond me," he thought.

At last, he sat under a tree and began to practice what he'd been taught, eventually attaining freedom and the joy that accompanies it. As he awakened, he saw why Mahākāśyapa had "fired" him. Not long after, he went back to see Mahākāśyapa, who held a big ceremony to celebrate Ananda's awakening, officially recognizing him as the second main lineage holder of the Buddha's teachings.

THREE STAGES OF PRACTICE

Our minds . . . are riddled by confusion and doubt.
> —Sogyal Rinpoche,
> *The Tibetan Book of Living and Dying,*
> edited by Patrick Gaffney and Andrew Harvey

According to most classical Buddhist texts, achieving this sort of freedom involves three stages: listening, contemplation, and meditation. The first two stages are not so very different from the elements of modern educational systems. "Listening" essentially means allowing oneself to be introduced to new facts or ideas, whether presented orally by a teacher or read in a book. During my travels I've met a number of teachers who have said that this phase of practice corresponds to an elementary stage of learning in which students are introduced to basic principles—for example multiplication tables, grammatical standards, or rules of driving.

"Contemplation," the second stage of practice, may sound mysterious; but essentially it involves thinking deeply about lessons learned through reading and oral teachings, and questioning whether or not what you've heard or read is a valid means of understanding and responding to life events. It probably doesn't take much contemplation to recognize that nine times nine actually equals eighty-one or that a sign on a street corner with the letters "S," "T," "O," "P" on a red background really does mean that you should apply your brakes and wait to see if there are any pedestrians crossing the street or cars approaching. But when it comes to larger issues, like considering whether, or how deeply, your life is colored or conditioned by discomfort or *dukkha*, then a bit more effort is necessary.

Contemplation of such larger issues can begin with simply asking, "Am I contented, right now, in my own skin? Am I comfortable in this chair, with these lights overhead, and with these sounds surrounding me?" No great analysis is required; there's no need to go into lengthy examination. It's a process of checking in with your sense of being alive, right here, right now.

Next, you can proceed to ask yourself about the thoughts and emotions that either occasionally or perhaps frequently cross your awareness. Do you sometimes experience shivers of regret over decisions you've made in the past? Do you experience feelings of anger or resentment toward people currently in your life or toward current personal or professional obligations?

Asking questions of this sort does not represent any sort of moral or ethical considerations. They're simply starting points for contemplating whether or not you experience discomfort on intellectual, emotional, or physical levels: whether or not your own experience corresponds to the basic insights of the Four Noble Truths. "Am I uncomfortable?" "Am I dissatisfied?" "Would I like something more out of life?" The words in which you frame such questions aren't particularly important. What you're looking at is what my teachers called the immediate or fresh essence of personal experience.

"Meditation," the third stage of practice, asks us to begin by simply observing our physical, intellectual, and emotional experiences without judgment. Nonjudgmental observation is the basis of meditation, at least in terms of the Buddhist tradition. Many cultures, of course, have developed their own specific forms of meditation practice, each uniquely suited to the cultural environment from which they emerged. Since my own training was grounded in the practices that have developed within the Buddhist tradition, I can't speak about the details of the practices that have evolved in other traditions and other cultures.

Although there are a variety of practices within the Buddhist tradition introduced by the Buddha and developed and refined over the centuries by great teachers in the countries where Buddhism has spread, the basis of these practices is nonjudgmental observation of experience. Even looking at a thought like, "Oh, I did such and such twenty years ago. How stupid of me to regret it, I was just a kid then!" is meditation. It's an exercise in simply observing thoughts, emotions, and sensations as they rise and fall in our experience.

And it *is* an exercise.

Some years ago, a Westerner came to Sherab Ling, where His

Eminence, Tai Situ Rinpoche—the head of the monastery and one of the most influential teachers of Tibetan Buddhism—was teaching about meditation and emptiness. Maybe the man was sleeping during the teachings on meditation or maybe his mind was drifting, but when Tai Situ Rinpoche began teaching about emptiness, he suddenly snapped to attention. "I need to get rid of *I*," he thought. "If I get rid of *I*, I'll realize emptiness. I'll be free. No more problems, no more suffering. So I'm going to stop saying *I*."

When he told Tai Situ Rinpoche about his solution, Rinpoche told him there was no benefit in that. "I" wasn't the problem. To recognize emptiness you have to look at the roots of "I"— ignorance, desire, and so on.

But the man didn't listen. He really believed his shortcut would work much faster and more effectively than any of the old methods the Buddha taught.

So he just stopped saying "I." Instead of saying, "I'm going to bed," he'd say, "Going to bed." If he was going to the nearby town of Beijnath, he would say, "Going to Beijnath." And after a year of doing this, he went crazy. He didn't experience emptiness. He didn't cut through the root causes of suffering. He just pretended he didn't exist.

I don't know what happened to him after he left Sherab Ling, but it was clear that his shortcut didn't work very well. In fact, it reflects a common misunderstanding about Buddhist teachings: that in order to find freedom, we have to get rid of what is often referred to nowadays as the "ego."

As I recently learned, however, ego is something of a mistranslation of what Sigmund Freud originally referred to as the conscious aspect of the mind. It is a set of functions that include decision making, planning, and analyzing information, which work together to achieve a balance among instinctive tendencies of desire and aversion, the memories, ideas, and habits impressed on us as children, and the conditions and events that occur in our environment. In his original writings, Freud referred to this collection of functions as the "I," a coherent sense of self that emerges from this delicate balancing act. The word "ego" was later substituted in translation in order to make his insights more acceptable to the scientific community of the mid-twentieth century.[1]

Over the years, ego and its related terms have accumulated a somewhat negative characterization. "Oh, that person is such an egotist!" people exclaim. Or maybe, "I'm sorry, I was just being egotistical." This somewhat negative connotation of ego has spilled over into many texts and translations of Buddhist teachings.

In terms of Buddhist philosophy, however, there is nothing inherently wrong or negative associated with experiencing or utilizing a sense of self or ego. The ego is simply a set of functions developed to assist us in navigating the domain of relative reality. We may as well condemn ourselves for having a hand or a foot. Difficulties arise when we become attached to the or ego as the *only* means through which we relate to our experience—a predicament comparable to relating to experience only in terms of our hands or feet. Most of us would probably agree that we aren't our hands or our feet; yet neither would we cut off our hands or feet because they aren't the sum total of who we are and what we're capable of experiencing.

[1]Bruno Bettelheim, *Freud and Man's Soul* (New York: Alfred A. Knopf, Inc.), 1982.

Likewise, though ego, "I," or "the sense of self" may persist on a somewhat more subtle level, there's no need to cut it off or cut it out. Rather, we can approach it as a tool—or, perhaps a collection of tools—through which we relate to experience.

Of course, we can't just wake up one morning and say, "Oh, today I'm going to look at the way I've understood everything for my entire life as just a temporary arrangement of interdependent possibilities." Wisdom has to be applied to be made a part of one's own life.

Most of us can admit that we feel discomfort to some extent or other, and that our experience is to some degree conditioned by our minds. But we tend to get a bit stuck at that point—either by trying to change our minds or by letting our thoughts, emotions, compulsions, and so on, simply take over.

A third alternative—the method or means proposed by the Buddha—is to simply look at the various thoughts, emotions, and so on, as various expressions of the infinite potential of the mind itself. In other words, to use the mind to look at the mind. That's a basic definition of what, in the Buddhist tradition, is commonly referred to as "meditation." As mentioned a while back, it is known in the Tibetan language as *gom,* "to become familiar with." Through meditation, we begin to become familiar with the mind.

The mind is so intimately related to the way we relate to ourselves and the world around us, however, that it's difficult to see at first. As one of my teachers put it, looking at the mind is like trying to see your own face without a mirror. You know you have a face and you may have some idea of what it looks like, but that idea is a bit hazy. Its features are obscured by layers of impressions that are constantly shifting, depending on our attitudes, emotions, and other conditions that affect our idea of our face.

Similarly, we know we have a mind, but its features are blurred by overlapping thoughts, feelings, and sensations; thoughts and feelings *about* our thoughts, feelings, and sensations; thoughts, feelings, and sensations *about* our thoughts about our thoughts, feelings, and so on. They all pile up on each other like cars crashing on a highway. "I've got to listen to this teaching on emptiness. I'm not listening hard enough. I'll never learn. Everyone else looks like they're listening and understanding. Why can't I? Well, maybe because my back hurts. And I didn't get much sleep last night. But that shouldn't matter, should it? My mind is emptiness, after all. This pain in my back is emptiness. But I don't get it. It doesn't seem like emptiness to me." And in the middle of all this, something completely unrelated might come up: "Where did I leave my cell phone?" or maybe a memory, "That stupid thing I said to so-and-so ten years ago—I still can't believe I said that," or even an urge, "I'd love a piece of chocolate right now."

The mind is always active: distinguishing, evaluating, and redistinguishing according to its evaluations—and reevaluating according to new or refined distinctions. More often than not, we find ourselves captivated by all this activity. It seems as normal and natural as looking through a window at the traffic on a busy street. Even if the street we live on isn't particularly busy, we still tend to look out the window to check the weather: Is it snowing? Raining? Is the sky cloudy or clear? Maybe we go from window to window to look out at our front yard, our backyard, the driveway on one side, or our neighbor's house on the other.

Caught up in the habit of looking through a window and defining experience in terms of what we see through it, we don't recognize that the window itself is what enables us to see. Turning the mind to look at the mind is like looking at the window rather than focusing exclusively on the scenery. In so doing, we begin very gradually to recognize that the window and what we see through it occur simultaneously. If we look out a window in one direction, for example, we'll see traffic, clouds, rain, and so on, in a particular way. If we look in a different direction, we'll see things a little differently: the clouds may seem closer or darker while cars and people may seem bigger or smaller.

If we take a step back, though, and look at the entire window, we can begin to recognize these limited, or directional, perspectives as different aspects of a much vaster panorama. There is an unlimited realm of passing thoughts, emotions, and sensations visible through our window, yet not affecting the window itself.

Twenty-five hundred years ago, the Buddha introduced a number of practices aimed at helping us to step back and observe the mind. In the following pages, we'll look at three of the most basic of these, which can be practiced anytime, anywhere, and by anyone—regardless of whether or not you consider yourself a Buddhist. Before doing so, however, it might be helpful to examine a few basic guidelines.

TAMING THE HORSE

> *For the mind to be still, the body must be disciplined.*
> —The Ninth Gyalwa Karmapa,
>   *Mahāmudrā: The Ocean of Definitive Meaning*,
>   translated by Elizabeth M. Callahan

As a young child, I loved to spy on my father and his students, especially when they were meditating. A deep sense of peace and steadiness flooded the tiny, wood-beamed room where he taught, no matter how many people crowded it (and it was often very crowded). Most people, I noticed, would be sitting in a certain way: legs crossed, hands resting in their laps or on their knees, backs straight, eyes half-closed, and mouths slightly open. Whenever I ran off to one of the caves in the mountains and pretended to meditate, I would try to imitate that position, even though I didn't understand why sitting one way or another was particularly necessary.

When I began receiving formal instructions, however, I was introduced to an analogy handed down through generations of Tibetan Buddhist teachers and students, comparing meditation practice to the relationship between a horse and rider. The "rider" is the mind, and the "horse" is the body. While a calm rider can soothe a restive horse, a steady horse can also calm a restive rider.

When we first begin to meditate, the mind is like a restive rider: sometimes agitated, jumping around between thoughts, emotions, and sensations. It is sometimes so overwhelmed by all this jumping around that it becomes dull, unfocused, or exhausted. So it's important, especially in the beginning, to seat ourselves on a steady horse, so to speak; to establish a physical posture that is simultaneously relaxed and alert. Too relaxed and the "horse" might just stop—preoccupied, maybe, by chewing grass. Too alert and the "horse" may become agitated by its surroundings or the mood or temperament of the rider. We need to find a physical balance: neither too relaxed (or "loose," as it is often described in Buddhist texts), nor too alert, nor too "tight." We need to tame the horse before we can begin to ride.

There's a formal method of taming and an informal way. The formal method is described in terms of seven "points" or physical positions. Over the centuries these have become known as the seven-point posture of *Vairochana*—a Sanskrit name or term that may be roughly translated as "illuminator" or "sun," an aspect of our capacity to "light up" in terms of experience rather than ideas or concepts.

The first "point" involves establishing a firm base or anchor that connects you to the environment in which you're practicing while providing a reference to the rest of your body. If possible, cross your legs so that each foot rests on the opposite leg. If you can't do this, you can just cross one foot on top of the opposite leg and rest your other foot beneath the opposite leg. If neither position is easy, you can just cross your legs. And if sitting cross-legged on the floor or a cushion—even on your couch or your bed—is difficult, you can just sit with your feet resting evenly on the floor or on a cushion. Don't worry if your feet or legs aren't positioned in exactly the same way as everyone else's in the room. The aim is to establish a physical foundation that is simultaneously comfortable and stable for you, as you are, here and now: not too tight, not too loose.

The second point is to rest your hands in your lap, with the back of one hand resting in the palm of the other. It doesn't matter which hand is placed on top, and you can switch their positions at any time. If you're practicing in a place that is warm and humid, for instance, the covered palm may get hot and sweaty after a while. If you're practicing somewhere cold, the top hand might start feeling a little numb or tingly. It's also fine to simply lay your hands palm-down over your knees. Of course, some people might have short arms and long legs, or long arms and short legs, which would make it difficult to rest the hands directly on the knees in either case. Some people might need to rest their hands above their knees while others might need to rest them below. However or wherever you rest your hands, the idea is to let them *rest*.

The third point is to allow some space between the arms and the upper body, lifting and spreading the shoulders a little bit. Many classic Buddhist texts describe this point as raising the shoulders so they "resemble the wings of a vulture"—a description often misunderstood as holding the shoulders somewhere up around your ears. Actually, that would be a rather tense and difficult position to maintain, especially for people who have broad or muscular arms that sit very closely to their upper bodies. "Where is there space? I can't find any space! Oh no, I have to make some space!"

The essence of the third point is to simply allow ourselves the opportunity to breathe. This may be understood on a literal level as the capacity to inhale and exhale, and on a figurative level as the ability to take in and let go of experience. More often than not, we sit, stand, and move around with our shoulders sagged or hunched, collapsing our lungs so we can't take a full, deep breath—and collapsing our awareness so that we can't absorb the full range of possible experience or let it go. Lifting and spreading the shoulders is like anticipating a deep breath or the possibilities of experience: a way of saying "Hello, breath! Hello, world! How are you today? Oh, now you're gone. But I'm sure you'll come back again."

The fourth point is to keep your spine as straight as possible, the ultimate physical expression of alertness: "I'm here! I'm awake! I'm alive!" But here, again, it's important to find a balance—not so stiff that you're practically bending backwards, but not so relaxed that you're slouching. You want to be, as the classic texts say, "straight as an arrow."

The fifth point involves the neck. Over the years of teaching around the world, I've noticed that certain cultural groups have developed some odd habits concerning this point. Asian students tend to forcefully bend their chins down toward their chests, frowning with tension, trying to hold everything in. They look like "meditation warriors," refusing to let any single thought disturb their minds. Western practitioners, meanwhile, tend to tilt their necks backwards, resting the back of their heads practically on top of their shoulders, exposing their throats and smiling broadly as if proclaiming to the world "I'm so peaceful and relaxed! My experience is so clear, so joyful, so full of bliss!" Tibetans—including myself—tilt their heads from side to side, causing their whole upper bodies to rock left to right and back again, apparently unable to find any comfortable alignment: "Maybe this way, maybe that way, I don't know."

The actual instruction is to lengthen the neck by tilting your chin slightly more toward your throat than you may ordinarily be used to doing while allowing yourself some freedom of movement. The sensation could be described as simply resting your head on your neck.

The sixth point concerns the mouth—the whole apparatus of lips, teeth, tongue, and jaws. If we look closely, we may find a habitual tendency to keep our lips, teeth, tongue, and jaws tightly clenched: *No way am I going to let anything pass in or out without my permission!* That doesn't mean we should force our mouths open, thinking *Now I'll have peace; now I'll be open.* Either way involves some tension. Rather, we can just allow the mouth to rest naturally as it does when we're at the point of falling asleep: maybe a little bit open, maybe totally closed, but not forced in either way.

The last of the seven points involves the eyes. People new to meditation sometimes find it easier to feel a sense of calmness or steadiness by keeping their eyes closed. This is fine at the beginning. One of the things I learned early on, though, is that keeping the eyes closed makes it easier to drift into such a relaxed state that the mind begins to wander or become a bit dull. Some people actually fall asleep. So after a few days of practice, it's better to keep your eyes open, so that you can stay alert and clear. This doesn't mean glaring straight ahead without blinking. This would be the opposite extreme of being too tight, like stiffening the spine so forcefully that it bends backwards. Simply leave your eyes open as they normally are throughout the day.

At the same time, it's best to maintain some sort of focus so that the eyes aren't wandering all the time, shifting around from experience to experience: *Oh, that person in front of me is blocking my view of Mingyur Rinpoche. Now who is that person walking in through the door? Where are those people whispering to each other while we're supposed to be meditating? Is that rain pounding against the window? Here comes my cat or dog. Where is it going? Does it want food or water?*

We don't have to be attached to a specific focus, though. Sometimes our focus can be a little bit downward, like staring down the nose. Sometimes it can be straight ahead. Sometimes it can be a little upward. The idea is to choose a focus, a steady visual perspective through which we can see many changes without being distracted by them.

There's also a short two-point posture, which can be adopted at times when it may be inappropriate (for example, while driving, making dinner, or grocery shopping) or physically impossible to assume the more formal seven-point posture. The points are simple: Keep your spine straight and your muscles loose. Like the seven-point posture, the two-point version fosters a balance between relaxation and alertness, neither too loose nor too tight, but somewhere in between.

Both approaches to "taming the horse" help to counteract the common tendency to slouch in a way that compresses the lungs and digestive organs, constricting the full range of our physical capacities. They also provide a physical reference point that can assist us in bringing our awareness back to the present moment of experience when the mind—the "rider"—drifts, wanders, or fixates on a particular point of view. I can say from personal experience that flopping down in the middle of a meditation session is a good way of bringing oneself back to the present moment. Recognizing tension in my muscles or other body parts has been quite useful in pointing out mental and emotional habits grounded in fear, desire, and other manifestations of attachment to a sense of "me" distinct from everything that is "not me."

Finding a physical equilibrium also helps to establish a balance between three aspects of experience, known in Sanskrit as *prana, nadi,* and *bindu,* and in Tibetan as *lung, tsa,* and *tigle. Prana* or *lung* refers to the energy that keeps things moving; *nadi* or *tsa* are the channels through which this energy moves; and *bindu* or *tigle* refers to "drops" or "dots" of vital essence propelled by energy through the channels. On a physical level, *bindu* or *tigle* may be compared, in very simple terms, to blood cells. *Nadi* or *tsa* could be compared to the arteries, veins, and capillaries through which the blood flows to the muscles and various organs. *Prana* or *lung* could be compared to the energy that propels the heart to pump blood through the intricate network of veins, arteries, and capillaries spread throughout our muscles and organs and draw it back again. *Prana, nadi,* and *bindu* all work together. If the *prana* is inconsistent, then the movement of *bindu* through the *nadi* is inconsistent. If the *nadi* are blocked or clogged, then the *prana* is inhibited and the movement of the *bindu* is constricted. If the *bindu* are conditioned—for example by an influx of adrenaline—they can't pass easily through the channels.

On a subtler level, *prana, nadi,* and *bindu* are various aspects of the mind: *bindu* is the aggregate of concepts ("me," "you," "what I like," "what I don't like"); *nadi* is the link between these concepts; and *prana is* the energy that keeps these concepts moving and flowing. There's a connection between the physical and subtle dimensions of *prana, nadi,* and *bindu.* If we can arrange the body in a way that balances its physical aspects, we open ourselves to the possibility of their subtle aspects. In other words, taming the "horse" provides a physical basis for taming the "rider."

TAMING THE RIDER

Rest like the movement of swells upon the sea.

—Jamgon Kongtrul Lodro Thaye,
Creation and Completion,
translated by Sarah Harding

The same principles behind finding a relaxed and alert physical posture apply to finding a balance within your mind: not too loose, not too tight. When your mind is poised naturally between relaxation and alertness, its potential spontaneously emerges.

A very simple analogy I use when I'm teaching is to show three different approaches to responding to being thirsty when a glass of water is sitting right in front of me.

First, I try struggling to reach for the glass, saying, "I've *got* to reach this glass. I've *got* to bring it to my lips. I've *got* to swallow some water or I'll die of thirst." But my hand, my arm, and my *intention* are all working so hard that I can't reach the glass four inches away from me and swallow. And even if I do manage to reach it, I'm shaking so hard that I'm more than likely to spill the water before it ever reaches my lips.

That's an example of being too tight: reaching so intensely for something that desperation inhibits fulfillment.

Next, I demonstrate the opposite extreme, barely lifting my hand, saying wearily, "Oh, I'd like some water, but I just don't *feel* like reaching for the cup. . . . It's too far away, and there's so much effort involved. Maybe I'll drink later. Maybe tonight. Maybe later."

That's an example of being too loose: not reaching for something because it just seems like too much work.

Finally, I demonstrate a middle way. "There's a cup of water," I say. "Just relax your hand, move it forward, pick up the glass, and drink."

Just as in the case of physical posture, the essential point of mental "posture" is to find a balance. If your mind is too tight or too focused, you'll end up becoming anxious over whether you're being a *good* meditator: *I've got to look at my mind. I've got to see the whole window. If I don't succeed, I'm a failure.* If your mind is too loose, you'll either get carried away by distractions or fall into a kind of dullness. *Oh, I probably should meditate, but it takes so much time. Yes, yes, there's a thought, there's a feeling, there's a sensation, but why should I care? It's just going to come around again.*

The ideal approach lies between these two extremes. *Hmm, there's a thought. There's a feeling. There's a sensation. Oh, now it's gone. Oh, now it's back. Oh, now it's gone again. Now it's back.*

We can treat these appearances and disappearances like a game, the way children sometimes look at clouds: "What do you see?" a child may exclaim. "I see a dragon!" one might respond.

Others might add their impressions. "I see a horse!" "I see a bird!" The cynic in the crowd may simply observe, "I don't see anything, just a cloud."

Especially at the beginning, it's important to keep the "game" short—playing, according to classical Buddhist texts, only as long as it takes to swallow a mouthful of food, drink a sip of tea, or take two or three steps across the room. Of course, just as there are many mouthfuls of food on a plate, many sips to drain a cup of tea, and many steps to cross a room, these short games can be repeated many times in one day.

Proceeding in this way, meditation becomes a part of your everyday life, rather than something you do because it's supposed to be "good for you." Over time you'll find it easier to maintain longer sessions—and look forward to whichever of the three basic practices you choose as interesting in itself rather than a duty to perform.

7

ATTENTION

To see the mountain on the other side, you must look at the mountain on this side.

—Dūsum Khyenpa, quoted in
Mahāmudrā: The Ocean of Definitive Meaning,
translated by Elizabeth M. Callahan

LEFT TO ITS own, the mind is like a restless bird, always flitting from branch to branch or sweeping down from a tree to the ground and then flitting up into another tree. In this analogy, the branches, the ground, and the other tree represent the demands we receive from our five senses, as well as thoughts and emotions. They all seem very interesting and powerfully attractive. And since there's *always* something going on in and around us, it's very hard for the poor restless bird to settle. No wonder so many of the people I meet complain of being stressed most of the time! This kind of flitting about while our senses are overloaded and our thoughts and emotions are demanding recognition makes it very hard to stay relaxed and focused.

The first of the basic practices to which I was introduced as a child—which most teachers introduce to beginning students—

involves allowing the little bird to settle. In Sanskrit, this practice is known as *shamatha* (the *th* is a slightly aspirated variant of *t*); in Tibetan, it is known as *shinay. Shama* and *shi* may be understood in a variety of ways, including "peace," "rest," or "cooling down" from a state of mental, emotional, or sensory excitement. Maybe a modern equivalent would be "chilling out." The Sanskrit *tha*, like the Tibetan *nay*, means to "abide" or "stay." In other words, *shamatha* or *shinay* means abiding in a state that is rested or "chilled out," which allows the little bird to just sit on one branch for a while.

Most of us, when we look at something, hear something, or watch a thought or emotion, have some sort of judgment about the experience. This judgment can be understood in terms of three basic "branches": the "I like it" branch, the "I don't like it" branch, or the "I don't know" branch. Each of these branches spreads out into smaller branches: "good" branch; "bad" branch; "pleasant" branch; "unpleasant" branch; "I like it because . . ." branch; "I don't like it because . . ." branch; "could be good or bad" branch; "could be nice or not" branch; "could be good *and* bad, pleasant *and* unpleasant" branch; and the "neither good nor bad, pleasant nor unpleasant" branch. The possibilities represented by all these branches tempt the little bird to flutter between them, investigating each one.

The practice of *shamatha* or *shinay* involves letting go of our judgments and opinions and just looking at, or paying attention to, what we see from whatever branch we're sitting on. Maybe we'll see a screen of branches and leaves. But instead of flitting from branch to branch to get a better view, just look at each branch or leaf, paying attention to its shape or color. Rest there on one branch. Attending to our experience in this way allows us to distinguish our judgments and opinions from the simple experience of seeing.

This practice has profound implications for the way we approach difficult emotions and the various problems we encounter in daily life. In most cases our experiences are conditioned by the branch we're sitting on and the screen of branches before us. But if we just look at our experience directly, we could see each branch and leaf as it is, and our opinions and judgments as they are—not all mixed up together, but as distinct aspects of experience. In that moment of pausing to just be aware, we open ourselves not only to the possibility of bypassing habitual ideas, emotions, and responses to physical sensation, but also to responding freshly to each experience as it occurs.

This simple awareness is an expression of the clarity of our buddha nature: the capacity to see and to recognize that we're seeing, but without any concepts attached or clouding our vision. We can recognize the concepts of "I like," "I don't like," and so on, as distinct from branches, leaves, or flowers. Because clarity is unlimited, we can hold all these different things at once without mixing them up. Actually, clarity is always functioning, even when we're not consciously attentive to it: when we become aware of being hungry or tired, when we recognize a traffic jam, or distinguish a chili pepper from a package of cheese. Without clarity, we wouldn't be able to think, feel, or perceive anything. *Shamatha* or *shinay* practice helps us to develop and appreciate our inherent clarity.

There are many ways to approach *shamatha* or *shinay* practice. Many of the people I've met over the years have asked for a step-by-step guide. "What should I do first?" they ask. "What should I do next?" In the following pages, I'll attempt to describe a step-by-step approach to each of the basic practices.

Step One: Objectless Attention

The most basic approach to attention is referred to as "object-less"—not focusing on any specific "scene" or aspect of experience, but just looking and marveling at the wide range of scenery as it comes and goes. During a recent trip to Rio de Janeiro, Brazil, I'd often exercise by hiking through a tall, nearby hill that was covered in a jungle-like forest of plants and trees bearing various types of fruit. Halfway up the hill, I'd get tired, overwhelmed by the heat and humidity, the altitude, and the sheer variety of foliage. But at certain places, there would be a wooden chair or bench. I'd sit in the chair and just rest, simply aware of my physical fatigue and my surroundings.

You don't have to hike through the hills of Rio de Janeiro to accomplish this sense of open relaxation and awareness. You can experience it after washing a big pile of dishes. When you've finished washing the dishes, you can sit down in a chair with a big sigh, "Ahh." Your physical body may be tired, but your mind is at peace, totally open, totally at rest, and immersed in the present moment of "Ahh." Maybe your children are making noise in another room or maybe you're watching TV—with all the changes in scenes and commercial interruptions. But neither disturbs your sense of "Ahh." Thoughts, feelings, and sensations may come and go, but you just observe them. You pay light and gentle—or what we in the Buddhist tradition refer to as "bare"—attention to them, as you rest with an "Ahh," simply open to the present moment. The past (washing dishes or climbing through a South American jungle) is over, and the future (more dishes, more jungles, bills to pay, or children to discipline) has yet to come. Right here, right now there is only the present "Ahh."

That's how to rest the mind in objectless attention: as though you've just finished a large, long, or difficult task. Just let go and relax. You don't have to block any thoughts, emotions, or sensations that arise, but neither do you have to chase them. Rest in the present moment of "Ahh." If thoughts, emotions, or sensations arise, simply allow yourself to be aware of them.

Objectless attention doesn't mean just letting your mind wander aimlessly among fantasies, memories, or daydreams. You may not be fixating on anything in particular, but you're still aware, still present to what's happening in the here and now. For example, while laid over recently in the Denver airport, I saw a lot of shuttle trains go by on a track overhead, taking people to different terminals and to different parts of each terminal. I sat there on my chair watching the trains go back and forth, content to observe them simply as appearances through my awareness. There was no need to get up and follow after every train, wondering, "Where is it going? Where is it coming from? How long will it take to get from where it started to where it ends up?" I just watched the trains go by.

When we practice on the level of objectless attention, we're actually resting the mind in its natural clarity, unaltered by the passage of thoughts, emotions, and physical sensations. This natural clarity is always present for us in the same way that space is always present. In a sense, objectless attention is like allowing ourselves to be aware of the branches and leaves in front of us while recognizing the space that allows us to *see* the branches and leaves in the first place. Thoughts, emotions, and sensations shift and quiver in awareness in the same way branches and leaves shift and quiver in space. Moreover, just as space isn't defined by the objects that move through it, awareness isn't defined or limited by the thoughts, emotions, and sensations it apprehends. Awareness simply *is*.

Objectless attention involves settling into this "is-ness," simply watching thoughts, emotions, appearances, and so on, as they emerge against or within the background of "space." Some people find the practice as easy as sitting in a chair after washing dishes; others find it rather difficult. I did. Whenever my father or other teachers tried to explain objectless attention, I was mystified and a little bit resentful. I couldn't understand how it was possible to just watch whatever was going on as if it were a movie, or, as the many Buddhist texts say, a "reflection of the moon in a puddle." In moments of greatest anxiety, my thoughts, feelings, and physical sensations didn't seem like reflections. They seemed terribly, solidly real. Fortunately, there are other steps we can take in order to guide us through the process of simply being aware.

Step Two: Attending to Form

As a consequence of being embodied beings, much of our experience is filtered through one or another of the five senses: sight, hearing, smell, taste, and touch. But since the five sense faculties—or *sense consciousnesses*, as most Buddhist texts refer to them—can only register sensory perceptions, Buddhist science describes a sixth sense, known as *mental consciousness*. This sixth sense—or sixth consciousness—shouldn't be confused with ESP, an ability to see into the future, or any other mysterious capability. It is more akin to what neuroscientists describe as the capacity to organize the information received through the senses and form a concept or mental image.

Mental consciousness is like the restless bird described earlier—flying from branch to branch, taking in the view, so to speak, from each branch. It tries to make sense of the information it receives and is impelled to respond. But it's possible to teach the bird to settle for a while by deliberately focusing its attention on one or another of the senses.

How?

In the course of ordinary experience, the mind already tends to fixate on sensory information. However, the information we receive through our senses is more often than not a source of distraction. Inasmuch as we're embodied beings, we would inevitably experience a sense of futility if we attempted to disengage completely from our senses or block the information we receive through them. The more practical approach is to make friends with this information and utilize it as a means of calming the mind.

As I was taught, this friendship is most easily established by focusing on the visual aspects of an object—for example, a rose. What we think or feel about it doesn't matter: "good rose," "bad rose," "I-don't-know rose." If we just look at it as it is, we can begin to separate our opinions from the simple experience of seeing. Our opinions aren't in themselves good or bad or confused. But when we collapse them together with an object, our minds become distracted. We start to wonder, "Is this a good rose or a bad rose? When was the last time I saw a rose?" The restless bird flies from branch to branch trying to "understand" the rose. Yet the rose itself is not to be understood, but merely seen.

The technical term for using the sense of sight as a means of resting the mind is "form meditation." Sounds a bit scary, doesn't it? Very strict and precise. Actually, form meditation is quite simple. In fact, we practice it unconsciously throughout the day, whenever we look at something like a television screen, a big pile of dirty dishes in the sink, or a person ahead of us at the grocery store. Form meditation simply involves raising this unconscious

149

process to the level of active awareness. Just by looking with bare attention at a specific object, the restless bird settles on its branch.

Whatever object you choose to look at—a rose, a TV screen, or the person ahead of you in the grocery store checkout line—you'll probably notice that it has two aspects: shape and color. Focus on whichever aspect you prefer. The focus itself doesn't matter: some people are more drawn to shapes, and others to colors. The idea is simply to rest your attention on either its color or its shape, engaging awareness only to the point of barely recognizing shape or color. It's not necessary to try to focus so intently that you take in every little detail. If you try to do that, you'll tense up, whereas the point of form meditation is to rest. Keep your focus loose, with just enough attention to hold a bare awareness toward whatever you're looking at. The visual object serves only as a reference point which allows your mind to settle, a cue for the little bird to stop fluttering from branch to branch—at least momentarily—and simply rest.

How to practice this method?

First, depending on your circumstances, assume whatever physical posture is most convenient or comfortable. Next, allow your mind to rest for a moment in objectless attention. Just observe all the thoughts, sensations, and so on, that come up. Then choose something to look at—the color of someone's hair, the shape of his or her haircut, or a rose, a peach, or your desktop—and just rest your attention on it, noticing its shape or color. You don't have to stare and if you need to blink, just blink. (In fact, if you don't blink, your eyes will probably become irritated and whatever you're looking at may appear irritating.) After a few moments of looking at someone or something, let your mind simply relax again in objectless attention. Return your focus to the object for a few moments; then allow your mind to relax once more.

Whenever I practice using a visual object as a support for resting the mind, I'm reminded of one of the earliest lessons I learned from my father. There is great benefit to be gained from alternating between object-based attention and the sort of objectless attention described earlier. When you rest your mind on an object, you're seeing it as something distinct or separate from yourself. But when we let go and simply rest our minds in bare attention, gradually we begin to realize whatever we see, and however we see it, is an image made up of thoughts, memories, and the limitations conditioned by our sensory organs. In other words, there's no difference between what is seen and the mind that sees it.

Step Three: Attending to Sound

Attending to sound is very similar to attending to form, except that now you're engaging the faculty of hearing instead of sight. Begin by taming your "horse" through assuming whatever posture is convenient, either the two-point posture or the seven-point one. Then take a few moments to "tame the rider" by resting in objectless attention, simply opening your awareness to whatever is going on without attaching to anything specific. Next, gradually allow yourself to pay attention to sounds close to your awareness, such as your heartbeat or your breath. Alternatively, you can focus on sounds that occur naturally in your immediate surroundings, such as rain pattering against a window, the noise of a television or stereo coming from a neighbor's apartment, the roar of an airplane passing above, or even the chirps and whistles of restless birds outside.

There's no need to try to identify these sounds, nor is it necessary to tune in exclusively to a specific sound. In fact, it's easier to let yourself be aware of everything you hear. The point is to cultivate a simple, bare awareness of sound as it strikes your ear. Like visual objects, sounds serve merely as a focus that allows the mind to rest.

As with form meditation, you'll probably find that you can focus on the sounds around you for only a few seconds at a time before your mind wanders off. That's not uncommon and is actually great! That wandering serves as a kind of cue (like flopping over on your meditation cushion) that you've become too loose or too relaxed. The horse has run off with the rider; or maybe the rider has run off on its horse. When you find your mind wandering, just bring yourself back to open attention and then turn your focus back to sounds once again. Allow yourself to alternate between resting attention on sounds and allowing your mind simply to rest in a relaxed state of open meditation.

One of the advantages of sound meditation lies in the capacity to assist us in gradually detaching from assigning *meaning* to the various sounds we hear. With practice, we can learn to listen to what we hear without necessarily responding emotionally to the *content*. As we grow accustomed to paying bare attention to sound simply *as* sound, we'll find ourselves able to listen to criticism without becoming angry or defensive and able to listen to praise without becoming overly proud or excited.

One young man who had been attending a large event at Sherab Ling came to me to discuss a problem he was having with sounds. "I'm very sensitive," he explained. "I need peace and quiet in order to practice. I've tried keeping my windows closed and using earplugs but noises still come through, and they disturb my concentration. It's especially hard at night with all the dogs barking." (There are a lot of wild dogs around the monastery, and they tend to bark a lot and fight one another and defend themselves against predators).

"I can't sleep," the man continued, "because, as I've mentioned, I'm extremely sensitive to sounds. I really wanted to join the group practice today, but I couldn't sleep. What can I do?"

I gave him instructions on sound meditation, using sounds as a means of focusing and calming the mind.

The next day, however, he came back to my room and told me, "Your instructions helped a little bit, but not much. Those dogs kept me up all night. As I've tried to explain, I'm really sensitive to sounds."

"Well," I told him, "there's not much I can do. I can't kill the dogs and I can't cure your sensitivity to sounds."

At that moment, the gong rang for *puja*, a kind of group ritual of devotion similar to the ceremonies performed in other religious traditions. A Tibetan *puja* is often accompanied by drums, horns, symbols, and group chanting, all of which can be quite loud. It's a cacophony that used to terrify me to the point of an anxiety or panic attack. But when I looked across the room, I saw the fellow who was "so sensitive" to sounds sitting near the back of the temple with his legs crossed and his body slumping forward. In the midst of the loudest, noisiest part of the *puja*, he was fast asleep.

At the end of the ceremony, we met at the door leading out of the temple. I asked him how it was possible that he could fall asleep during all that noise and commotion.

He thought about it for a moment and then replied, "I guess because I didn't resist the sounds. They were just a part of the *puja*."

"Maybe you were just tired after so many nights of not sleeping," I suggested.

"No," he replied, "I think I've just learned that my sensitivity to sound was a kind of a story I kept telling myself, an idea that got stuck in my head, perhaps when I was a child."

"So what are you going to do tonight?" I asked.

He smiled. "Maybe I'll listen to the dogs and hear it as their kind of *puja*."

The next day, he came to the room and announced proudly that he'd slept like a baby. "I think," he said, "I may have lost my attachment to the idea that I'm overly sensitive to sounds."

I like this story because it demonstrates an important principle. We're disturbed by sensations to the degree that we resist them. This young man, after some practice, discovered that the sounds we hear are like the music of a universal *puja*: a celebration of our capacity to hear.

Step Four: Attending to Physical Experience

Chances are that if you're reading this book, you live, so to speak, in a physical body. On some level, we tend to regard embodiment as something of a limitation. Wouldn't it be nice to just float freely without the constraints of physical needs and demands, without the demands of ignorance, desire, or aversion? But our embodied state is a blessing in disguise, fertile ground through which we may discover the possibilities of awareness.

One way to access these possibilities is through paying attention to physical sensations, a process that may be most simply accessed through watching your breath. All you have to do is focus your attention lightly on the simple act of inhaling and exhaling. You can place your attention on the passage of air through your nostrils or on the sensation of air filling and exiting your lungs.

Focusing on the breath is particularly useful when you catch yourself feeling stressed or distracted. The simple act of drawing attention to your breath produces a state of calmness and awareness that allows you to step back from whatever problems you might be facing and respond to them more calmly and objectively. If you're overwhelmed by situations, events, vivid thoughts, or strong emotions, simply bring your attention to the simple sensation of breathing. No one will notice that you're meditating. They probably won't even pay attention to the fact that you're breathing at all!

There's also a more formal way to use the physical sensation of breathing as a focus for settling the mind, which I found very useful very early on in my training, especially when panic or anxiety threatened to take over. Whether resting in the seven-point posture or the two-point posture, simply count your inhalations and exhalations. Count the first inhalation and exhalation as "one," the next inhalation and exhalation as "two," and so on, until you reach twenty-one. Then just start the process again from "one."

Using breath as a focus can be extended to other aspects of physical experience. A lot of people I've met over the past several years live in constant physical pain, maybe as a result of an accident or a chronic illness. Understandably, the pain they experience makes it hard to concentrate on anything *but* the pain. But the pain itself can become a focal point that leads to a broader awareness of pain as an expression of the mind.

I saw this potential as I watched my father die. Pain wracked his body to the point where he couldn't void his bladder or bowels without assistance. But he approached each moment of pain as a revelation, a focus of awareness through which his mind became more relaxed and stable. Even in his last moments, he looked at the process of numbness in his arms and limbs, the congestion in his lungs, and the cessation of his heartbeat with a kind of child-like wonder, as if to say: "These experiences are neither good nor bad. They're just what's happening in the present moment." Even in the extremis of death, whatever his physical experiences, he took them as opportunities to rest his mind.

He was fortunate insofar as he'd had a lot of practice in working with physical sensation as a focus for resting the mind. But watching him die brought back some of the earliest lessons he'd taught me about working with physical sensation as a basis for resting the mind—in other words, relying on physical sensation and relating to it not as a threat or an enemy, but rather as an opportunity to become aware of awareness.

As with other attention practices, it's best to begin by seating yourself in a steady posture and resting for a few moments in objectless *shinay*. Then turn your attention gently to the physical sensation in a specific area: your neck, your knees, your hands, or your forehead. Sensation in any of these areas may already be apparent, but our ordinary tendency is to avoid it, resist it, or attend to it as the defining condition of our experience. Instead, slowly bring your attention to this area of your body.

Maybe you'll feel a sort of tingling or warmth or perhaps some pressure. Whatever you feel, just allow yourself to be aware of it for a moment or two. Just notice it, gently resting your attention on the sensation without qualifying it as good or bad, pleasant or unpleasant. It is what it is, as it is. Slowly, through examining physical sensation in this way, you can begin to recognize that your opinions and judgments about the sensation are contributory factors, interpretations overlaid upon the simple awareness of sensation in itself. After a moment, let go of your attention to physical sensation and let your mind rest as it is. Then return your attention to your physical sensations.

Once you've spent a little time resting your awareness on the sensations in one part of the body, you can extend the process by gently drawing your attention throughout your entire body. In this process I sometimes refer to physical sensations as "scanning practice," because it reminds me of lying in one of those MRI and *f*MRI machines that can scan your entire body. In this case, however, the scanner isn't some external machine, but your own mind, your own awareness.

When I first began to practice attention on the level of physical sensation, I discovered that when I tried to avoid a particular sensation, its power to affect me increased. I was actively participating in what was occurring right then, at that moment. I was struggling with my own awareness. My attention was divided between resisting a painful sensation and being overwhelmed by it. Through the guidance of my teachers, I began to observe these conflicting impulses simultaneously. I slowly—and by no means easily—began to see my whole mind engaged in a kind of battle between avoidance and acceptance. The process of observing this battle became more interesting than taking sides in the battle. Just watching it gradually became fascinating in itself.

Physical sensations like being cold, hot, hungry, full, heavy, or dizzy—or having a headache, a toothache, a stuffy nose, a sore throat, pain in your knees or lower back—tend to be directly present to awareness. Inasmuch as pain and discomfort are experienced so vividly, they're actually very effective means of focusing on the mind that is *aware* of pain: no pain, no awareness of the *mind that experiences* pain.

This is not to say that we should think that paying attention to pain will make the pain go away. If we do that, we're enhancing the power of hope and fear: hope that the pain will go away and fear that it won't. The best method is to observe the mind that experiences pain, which isn't always easy. In fact, the practice of attending to painful sensations is tricky. Sometimes the pain we feel may shift between various parts of the body. Sometimes it disappears altogether, in which case there's no support for meditation. Sometimes the sensation of pain can become so intense that it becomes overwhelming. Especially in the latter two cases, stop focusing on pain. Shift to some other focus, like sight or sound. Or just stop looking and do something completely different—take a walk, if you're able, or read a book, or watch TV.

Of course, if you're experiencing chronic or serious pain, it's important to consult a doctor. These symptoms may indicate a serious physical problem that requires medical treatment. Attention to pain doesn't mean that its physical causes go away. If your doctor has uncovered a serious medical problem, by all means follow his or her recommendations. Although attention to painful physical sensations can assist us in dealing with the pain or discomfort of serious medical problems, it's not a substitute for treatment.

Even while taking medications prescribed or recommended by a doctor, you may experience some pain. In this case you can try working with the physical sensation of pain as a support for meditation. If the pain you experience is a symptom of a serious medical condition, avoid focusing on results. If your underlying motivation is to get rid of the pain, you're actually reinforcing the mental and emotional habits associated with hope and fear. The best way to relinquish fixation on these habits is to simply make the effort to observe the pain objectively, leaving results to sort themselves out.

Step Five: Attending to Thoughts

Working with the activity of sensory perceptions is kind of a preparation for working with the restless bird itself—the multitude of ideas, judgments, and concepts that provoke the bird to jump from branch to branch. Thoughts are a bit more elusive than flowers, sounds, or physical sensations. At first, they rush and tumble, like water rushing over a cliff. You can't really see them. But by paying attention to them, in the same way that you pay attention to sounds or visual objects, you can come to an awareness of their passage. In so doing, you can become aware of the mind through which all these thoughts appear and disappear. "Thinking," as my father used to say, "is the natural activity of the mind, an expression of the mind's capacity to produce anything."

Paying attention to thoughts isn't aimed at stopping thoughts, but at simply observing them. Like taking time to look at a rose or to listen to a sound, taking time to observe your thoughts doesn't involve analyzing the thoughts themselves. Rather, the emphasis rests on the act of observing, which naturally calms and steadies the mind that observes. You can *use* your thoughts rather than being used *by* them. If a hundred thoughts pass through your mind in the space of a minute, you have a hundred supports for meditation. If the restless bird jumps from branch to branch, that's terrific. You can just watch the bird flitting around. Each leap, each burst of flight is a support for meditation.

There's no need to become attached to the awareness of a thought or to focus on it so intently that you attempt to make it go away. Thoughts come and go, as an old Buddhist saying holds, like "snowflakes falling on a hot rock." Whatever passes through the mind, just watch it come and go, lightly and without attachment, the way you'd practice gently resting your attention on forms, sounds, or physical sensations.

For most of us, thoughts seem very solid, very true. We become attached to them or afraid of them. Either way, we give them power over us. The more solid and true we believe them to be, the more power we give to them. But when we begin to observe our thoughts, the power begins to fade.

Sometimes if you watch your thoughts, you'll start to notice that they appear and disappear quite quickly, leaving little gaps between them. At first the gap between one thought and the next may not be very long. But with practice the gaps grow longer and your mind begins to rest more peacefully and openly in objectless attention. Sometimes, the simple practice of observing thoughts becomes something like watching TV or a movie. On the screen, lots of things may be going on, but you are not actually *in* the movie or on the TV. There's a little bit of space between yourself and whatever you're watching. As you practice observing your thoughts, you can actually experience that same little bit of space between yourself and your thoughts. You're not really creating this space; it was always there. You're merely allowing yourself to notice it.

Whichever of these experiences comes up for you is okay, and no doubt your experiences will vary as you practice. Sometimes you'll observe your thoughts quite closely, seeing them come and go, and noticing the gaps between them. Sometimes you'll simply watch them with that little bit of distance. Practice—or method— is so much easier than most people think. Whatever you experience, as long as you maintain awareness of what's going on, *is* practice. That *is* the transformation of understanding into experience.

The only point at which observing thoughts shifts from meditation into something else occurs when you try to control or change your thoughts. But even if you bring some awareness to your attempt to control your thoughts, that's practice, too. It's *your* mind you're working with, so no one can judge you, no one can grade you on your experience. Practice is personal. No two people's experiences are alike.

If you continue, you'll inevitably discover that your own experience shifts sometimes from day to day and moment to moment. Sometimes you may find your thoughts are very clear and easy to observe. Sometimes they rush by like water flowing over a cliff. At other times, you may find your mind is dull or foggy. That's fine. You can simply observe the dullness or the agitation. Giving bare attention to whatever your experience is at any given moment *is* practice or method. Even thoughts like "I can't meditate," "my mind is too restless," "I'm so tired, do I *have* to meditate?" can be a support for meditation as long as you observe them.

Especially if you're new to meditation, it can be very difficult to simply observe thoughts associated with unpleasant experiences or vivid emotional content. This is especially true if those thoughts are related to long-standing beliefs: that we'll always be lonely, will never be attractive, or that an authority figure—whether a parent, a partner, or a manager at work—is an "enemy," always holding us down in some way. Particularly when thoughts are unpleasant, it's best to avoid focusing on the *object* of these thoughts—the argument, the content of unpleasant memories, or the chain of events that led to the formation of certain thoughts. Just look at the thoughts themselves, rather than the causes and conditions from which they emerge.

There's an old, old story drawn from the *sutras,* in which the Buddha compared the futility of looking for the causes and conditions that give rise to certain thoughts to a solider who'd been shot by a poisoned arrow on the battlefield. The doctor comes to remove the arrow, but the solider says, "Wait, before you pull out the arrow, I need to know the name of the person who shot me, the village he came from, and the names of his parents and grandparents. I also need to know what kind of wood the arrow is made from, the nature of the material the point is made of, and the type of bird that the feathers attached to the arrow were taken from. . ." on and on. By the time the doctor had investigated all these questions and returned with answers, the soldier would be dead. This is an example of self-created suffering, the kind of intellectual overlay that inhibits us from dealing with painful situations simply and directly.

The moral of the story is to let go of the search for reasons and stories, and simply look at experience directly. Extract the poison arrow of pain right now and ask questions later. Once the arrow is removed, the questions are irrelevant.

The best way to work with thoughts is to step back and rest your mind in objectless *shinay* for a minute and then bring your attention to each thought and the ideas that revolve around it. Observe both directly for a few minutes, just as you would observe the shape or color of a form. Then rest in the simple awareness of bare attention, alternating between attention to thoughts and the broader field of objectless attention. In this way, you avoid clinging too tightly to observing thoughts, while renewing the observation of thoughts with greater openness and freshness.

Begin by aligning your body in a posture that is relaxed and alert. Next, rest in objectless attention for a few moments. Then start watching your thoughts. Don't try to practice for very long—only a few minutes—alternating between objectless attention and attention to your thoughts.

Rest your mind for a moment in objectless attention. . . .

Watch your thoughts for maybe a minute. . . .

Then rest your mind in objectless attention. . . .

At the end of the process, ask yourself what the experience of observing your thoughts was like. Did thoughts rush by like water running over a cliff? Were you able to see your thoughts very clearly? Were they blurry and indistinct? Did they just vanish as soon as you tried to look at them? Did you experience any gaps?

No matter what you experience, the *intention* to observe *is* practice. Your thoughts might rush over a cliff; they may be blurry or indistinct; or they may be a bit shy and not appear at all. But your intention to watch these varieties of experience will, in time, shift your relationship to them.

Step Six: Attending to Emotions

Emotions are often vivid and enduring. But those same qualities can be very useful as supports for practice. Intensity and persistence can, in themselves, become a focus for looking at the mind. At the same time, those same characteristics of intensity and persistence can make it a bit difficult to work with emotions right away. Sometimes an emotion or an emotional tendency persists on such a deep level of awareness that we don't easily recognize its conditioning effect. That's why it's important to work with the first few steps of attention training first. In so doing, you can gain some familiarity with stabilizing awareness to the point at which you can observe whatever passes through your mind without too much attachment or aversion.

Early on in my own training, my father and my other teachers impressed on me that there are three very basic categories of emotion: positive, negative, and neutral. Each corresponds to the three main boxes through which we view ourselves and our experience: the "I like" box, the "I don't like" box, and the "I don't know" box.

"Positive," or what we might call "constructive," emotions, like compassion, friendship, and loyalty, strengthen the mind, build our confidence, and enhance our ability to assist those in need of help. "Negative" emotions such as fear, anger, sadness, jealousy, and envy tend to weaken the mind, undermine confidence, and increase fear. As such, they are often referred to as "destructive." More or less neutral states, meanwhile, basically consist of the kinds of attitudes we might have toward a pencil, a piece of paper, or a paper clip.

The method of observing emotions as supports for practice varies according to the type of emotion you're experiencing. If you're feeling a positive emotion, you can focus on both the feeling *and* the object of the feeling. For example, if you're feeling love for a child, you can rest your attention on both the child *and* the love you feel for him or her. If you're feeling compassion for someone in trouble, you can focus on the person needing help *and* your feeling of compassion. In this way, the object of your emotion becomes a support for the emotion itself, while the emotion becomes a support for focusing on the object that inspires the emotion.

On the other hand, holding an object of negative emotion in attention tends to reinforce an idea of that person, situation, or thing as the *cause* of a negative emotion. No matter how much you try to cultivate compassion, confidence, or any other positive feeling, you'll almost automatically associate the object with the negative emotion. "That person (or situation, or thing) hurts. Resist it. Try to change it. Run away."

I've also seen this tendency sometimes when people talk about someone toward whom they feel a romantic attraction. They feel this attraction quite strongly, but the more they try to pursue the other person, the more the other person tends to turn away. So the person who is attracted begins to feel that there is something wrong or unattractive about him- or herself. Or the person to whom he or she is attracted is cruel, unreliable, or flawed in some way essential to his or her nature. In fact, there's nothing wrong or bad about the person who is attracted and the person toward whom one is attracted. They're both expressing the infinite capacity of their buddha nature: to be attracted or not, to desire and not to desire. But we tend to take these expressions personally, as a way of defining ourselves and our relationships.

A more practical approach to emotions, similar to that of working with thoughts, is simply to rest your attention on the emotion itself rather than on its object. Just look at the emotion without analyzing it intellectually. Don't try to hold on to it or resist it. Simply observe it. When you do this, the emotion won't seem as solid, lasting, or true as it initially did.

Sometimes, though, the object associated with a disturbing

emotion—a person, a place, or an event—is just too vivid or present to ignore. If that's the case, by all means don't try to block it. Rest your attention on the sensory perceptions related to the object of your emotion, according to the methods of attention discussed earlier. In so doing, the object of emotion can become as powerful a support for meditation as the emotion itself.

So let's begin to use the method of attention to observe emotions. Keep your practice short—continuing perhaps for only a minute or two, shifting between objectless attention and attention to your emotions.

Start by "taming your horse," positioning your body in a way that is relaxed and alert. Next, rest in objectless attention for a few moments. Then bring your attention to whatever emotion you're feeling. You may be experiencing more than one emotion at the same time, of course, so let your attention be drawn simply to the one that is most vivid at the moment. Inasmuch as certain emotions like jealousy, frustration, anger, or desire may be particularly intense, it's important to just look at them lightly. Don't try to analyze them or figure out why or how they came about. The main point is to simply allow yourself to become aware of them.

Rest your mind for a moment in objectless attention. . . .

Watch your emotions for maybe a minute. . . .

Then rest your mind in objectless attention. . . .

At the end of the process, ask yourself what the experience of observing your emotions was like. Did they persist? Did they change? Were they very clear? Did they just hide when you tried to look at them? Did you experience any gaps between one emotion and another? Were they predominantly constructive or destructive?

As we look at our emotions in this way we begin to see the potential for every type of emotion as a basis for recognizing the mind that is aware of emotions. Sometimes we act out on them. In the case of positive or constructive emotions, as we shall discover, the beneficial effects can be immense, not only for ourselves but for those around us. Most of us, however, are caught up in some sort of mix between constructive and destructive emotions. These tendencies are more often than not layered, like the different layers of rock in a wall of the Grand Canyon. The benefit of looking directly at each layer lies in recognizing that each is an expression of our capacity to *see*.

The next set of practices offers a means of working with these layers to cut through their seeming solidity.

8

INSIGHT

*After concentrated intellectual activity, the intuitive
mind seems to take over and can produce the sudden
clarifying insights which give so much joy and delight.*

—Fritjof Capra

IT USED TO be fairly common for Buddhist practitioners to meditate in charnel grounds—areas covered with human bones and decaying corpses. They would spend nights, which some consider
the most frightening and uncertain hours, during which sights,
even under a full moon, are unclear, and sounds, like the rattling
of wind rustling through bones or the wailing of a dog, can't be
readily indentified. The aim of their practice was to confront their
own attachment to their bodies, desires, hopes, and fears, and gain
a deep experience of impermanence and emptiness.

I recently heard of one monk who'd gone to a charnel ground in
India and staked a *phurba*—a ritual knife representing stability of
awareness—into the ground in front of a heap of bones. He sat
quietly looking at the bones, meditating on the impermanence of
life and the emptiness from which all experiences arises. Then he
heard a noise nearby, a howling that frightened him. He started to

run away; but somehow, in the dark, he'd stuck his *phurba* through the hem of his robes, anchoring him to the ground. He couldn't run, he couldn't move, and he was terrified. "This is it," he thought. "I'm going to die now."

An instant later, he realized, "That's what I came here to learn." There was no "me," no "I," and no monk—just a pile of bones surrounded by decaying flesh moved by ideas, emotions, and physical sensations. He pulled up his *phurba* and walked home to his monastery, but with a deeper experience of emptiness.

This doesn't mean that in order to understand emptiness and impermanence you have to go to a cemetery, stick a knife in your pant cuffs, skirt hem, or shoe, and experience terror over not being able to move. We experience enough terror—as well as uncertainty, attachment, aversion—in our daily lives: at work, in relationships, and watching children go off to school. The question is, Who is experiencing terror? Who is uncertain? Where does desire—or jealousy, confusion, loneliness, or despair—*live*? Where do these various identities—mother, child, employee, boss, and so on—come from? Where do they go when they pass? Where do they exist when we experience them?

FROM CONCEPT TO EXPERIENCE

> *Just realizing the meaning of mind*
> *Encompasses all understanding.*
> —Jamgon Kongtrul Lodrö Thaye,
> *The Outline of Essential Points,*
> translated by Maria Montenegro

Understanding is like a map. It shows us where we need to go and the directions for how to get there. A map, however, is not the journey. The intellectual understanding of emptiness that comes from breaking things down into smaller and smaller parts, acknowledging impermanence and interdependence (as described earlier), is what we might call "analytical meditation." On an analytical level, it may be obvious that "I" am not my foot or my hand or my brain. But that level of analytical contemplation represents the first step of the journey.

I've heard that some people, upon hearing about emptiness, immediately recognize that cherished notions of "self" and "other," the "I like" box, the "I don't like" box, the "I don't know" box, and all the smaller boxes within them dissolve instantly. I was not one of those fortunate few. For me, it's taken effort, which is still ongoing. There are boxes within boxes yet to be discovered. Attaining some stability in experiencing the union of clarity and emptiness evolves over time.

Over the years, however, I've learned that this gradual process of unfolding isn't an obstacle but an opportunity to discover deeper and deeper levels of awareness. How can you impose limits on what is essentially unlimited?

Fortunately, I was taught a means or method of cutting through concepts to arrive, even momentarily, at a direct experience of emptiness unified with clarity. This method is known in Sanskrit as *vipashyana* and in Tibetan as *lhaktong*. The traditional translation of these terms is "insight," though the actual words mean something closer to "superior seeing" or "seeing beyond."

What are we seeing beyond? All our concepts: "me" and "mine," "them" and "theirs," and the often scary, very solid notions about "reality."

Vipashyana or *lhaktong* is not merely an intellectual exercise. It's a gut-level practice, rather like feeling your way through a completely dark room to find the door. With every blind step you take, you ask, "Where is me?" or "Where is anger?" or "Who is the person I'm angry with?"

Combining the understanding of emptiness with the method of attention, *vipashyana* or *lhaktong* offers an experiential method of cutting through conceptual attachments to "me," "mine," "you," "yours," "them," "theirs," "anger," "jealousy," and so on. We come face-to-face with the freedom of awareness unlimited by mental and emotional habits.

Though we're conditioned to identify with the thoughts that pass through our awareness rather than with awareness itself, the awareness that is our true nature is infinitely flexible. It is capable of any and every sort of experience—even misconceptions about itself as limited, trapped, ugly, anxious, lonely, or afraid. When we begin to identify with that timeless, pristine awareness rather than with the thoughts, feelings, and sensations that pass through it, we've taken the first step toward facing the freedom of our true nature.

One student expressed it this way: "When I was going through my divorce, I worked very hard at being aware of the pain I was experiencing. I broke it down into little pieces, looking at the thoughts that came up in my mind and the sensations that occurred in my body. I thought a lot about the pain my soon to be ex-husband must be experiencing and the pain that other people in our situation were probably feeling, and realized I wasn't alone. And the idea of what they might be going through without the benefit of looking at their sorrow, anxiety, or whatever made me want them to feel better.

"Working with the pain in this way, I gradually came to experience—not just intellectually, but on an intuitive, 'Yes, this is how it is' sort of way—that *I* was *not* my pain. Whoever or whatever *I* was, was an observer of my thoughts and feelings and the physical sensations that often accompanied them. Of course I experienced grief or loneliness at times, felt some heaviness around my heart or in my stomach, wondered if I'd made a terrible mistake, and wished I could turn time backwards. But as I looked at what was passing through my mind and body, I realized that there was someone—or something—bigger than these experiences. That something was the 'looker,' a presence of mind that wasn't disturbed by my thoughts, feelings, and sensations, but just observed them all without judging whether they were good or bad.

"Then I started looking for the 'looker,' and I couldn't find her! It wasn't as if there was *nothing* there—there was still this sense of awareness—but I couldn't put a name to it. Even 'awareness' didn't seem to fit. It seemed too small a word. For just a couple of seconds, maybe more, it was like the 'looker,' the looking, and what was being looked at were all the same.

"Oh, I know I'm not saying this very well, but there was just a sense of bigness. It's so hard to explain. . . ."

Actually, she explained it very well—or as well as she could, since the experience of emptiness can't really fit neatly into words. A traditional Buddhist analogy for this experience compares it to giving candy to a mute: someone who tastes the sweetness of candy but can't describe it. In modern terms, we might refer to the experience in terms of the "innocent perspective" mentioned earlier, in which we're confronted by a panorama so vast there is simply the awareness of seeing: for an instant there's no distinction between the "seer," what is "seen," and the act of seeing.

We sometimes experience this innocent perspective accidentally on waking up in the morning. For a second or two there's disorientation, during which we can't attach any concepts to who is seeing, what is being seen, or the act of seeing. During those few moments, there's simply awareness, a nonconceptual openness that transcends "here," "now," "this," or "that."

Then the habits of relative perspective rush in and we begin to think, "Oh, yes, I am me. That is my husband (or wife or partner or dog or cat) beside me on the bed. Those are the walls of the bedroom, the ceiling, the windows, and the curtains. That's a lamp on a nightstand beside the bed. There's a dresser over there. . . ." At the same time, our thoughts and feelings *about* ourselves, about the room, about the day ahead of us or the days behind us, about the people we're likely to meet or like to meet, about the people we've lost, and so on, emerge. Quite unconsciously, we engage in the process of making distinctions. Sometimes slowly, sometimes quickly we begin to grasp at them as determining and reinforcing points of reference for navigating our inner and outer worlds.

Clinging to these distinctions as absolute rather than relative is probably the most basic description of the Sanskrit term *samsara*, which in Tibetan is referred to as *khorlo*. Both terms may be understood as spinning around on a wheel that keeps turning and turning in the same direction. We have the sense of motion and a sense of change, but actually we're just recycling the same old mental and emotional patterns in different forms.

Release from this sort of mental and emotional recycling is commonly referred to in Sanskrit as *nirvana* and in Tibetan as *nyang-day*. Both terms refer to the realization, through direct experience, of our inherently free nature—a perfect peace of mind free from concepts, attachment, aversion, and so on. A common misperception of the Buddha's teaching, however, is that in order to attain *nirvana,* we have to deny *samsara*—evade it, get rid of it, get out of it. *Samsara* is the enemy! *Samsara* is the boss!

Samsara is neither enemy nor boss. Nor is it a "place," a common misinterpretation of the term. *Samsara* may be more accurately understood as a point of view to which we've become attached in an effort to define ourselves, others, and the world around us as we travel a realm characterized by impermanence and interdependence.

However uncomfortable, *samsara* is at least familiar. *Vipashyana,* or insight practice, may seem difficult or even uncomfortable at first because it disturbs our attachment to what is familiar. To use a very simple analogy, imagine your experience as a piece of paper that has been rolled up for a long time. You can try to straighten the paper out to its entire length, but it will most likely tend to roll back up. In order to see the entire piece of paper, you'd have to anchor it down on both edges. Then you can see the whole paper instead of just a few of the words written on it. There's a lot more to see than the few words we're used to reading.

Now imagine that the paper just keeps unrolling—there's no end to it! The words are not the paper, nor is the act of reading the words on the paper. They all occur simultaneously: the words, the paper, and reading the words on the paper.

This is only an analogy, of course, but perhaps it may help to explain that the appearances of *samsara,* and even our attachment to them, are only possible because the basis of our experience is *nirvana*—the capacity to experience anything joined with our capacity to perceive whatever appears. *Samsara* is an expression of *nirvana,* just as relative reality is an expression of absolute reality. We just need to practice recognizing that even our attachment to certain reference points of relative reality is possible because of the union of emptiness and clarity.

As with *shinay* or *shamatha* practice, there are certain steps we can take in order to arrive at insight, the direct experience of clarity and emptiness. I won't say that the process of developing such direct experience is simple or easy. In fact, it should be undertaken very slowly, mouthful by mouthful, sip by sip. There's no quick and easy means to overcoming mental and emotional habits that have accumulated over a lifetime. But the journey itself provides its own rewards.

So now let's look at the process.

The Empty "I"

Who am I?

This question haunts us, most frequently on a subtle level, throughout almost every moment of our daily lives. Try as we might, we can't really find an "I," though, can we? Our opinions shift and our relationships to others reflect different aspects of "I." Our bodies are going through constant changes. So we begin by looking for an inherent "I" that can't be defined by circumstances. We act is if we had an "I" to protect, avoiding pain and seeking comfort and stability. When pain or discomfort occurs, we seek to remove ourselves from it, and when something pleasant occurs, we seek to attach ourselves to it. The implication here is that pain and pleasure, comfort and discomfort, and so on, are somehow extraneous to this "I."

Oddly enough, however deeply we may observe our responses,

we don't have a very clear picture of what this "I" really is. Where is it? Does it have a definite shape, color, or any other physical dimension? What can you say about "I" that is permanent or unconditioned by experience?

Transcending this experience of "I" doesn't involve speculating about whether or not "I" truly exists. Such speculation may be interesting in a philosophical sense, but it doesn't offer much help in dealing with moment by moment experience. The practice of insight involves examining ourselves in terms of our investment in an "I" existing independently of circumstances as a valid reference point of experience.

In order to begin this examination, it's of course essential to assume a physical posture that is relaxed and alert. Next, rest your mind using the practice of objectless attention described earlier. Then look for "I"—the one who is observing the passage of thoughts, emotions, sensations, and so on.

At first, this process may involve some sort of analysis.

Is "I" my hand?

My foot?

Is "I" the discomfort I may be feeling with my legs crossed?

Is "I" the thoughts that occur or the emotions I feel?

Are any of these "I"?

Then we can turn from this analytical process to look for "I."

Where is "I"?

What is "I"?

Don't keep this investigation going very long. The temptation to arrive at a conceptual or a philosophical position is quite strong. The point of the exercise is simply to allow yourself to discover within your own experience a sense of freedom from the idea of "I" as permanent, singular, and independent. Emptiness, as discussed earlier, isn't a decision we make about the nature of absolute reality or an awareness attained through analysis or philosophical argument. It's an experience, which, once tasted, can change your life, opening new dimensions and possibilities. That is the point of insight practice.

The Empty "Other"

Joining *shamatha* or *shinay* with an understanding of emptiness doesn't mean denying relative reality. Relative reality is the framework within which we operate in this world, and denial of that framework—as seen in the case of the fellow who simply stopped saying "I"—is the path of madness. But there's a third level of experience which I call "fake relative reality." In it, ideas, feelings, and perceptions are intimately bound up in our perception of ourselves, other people, sensations, and situations. Fake relative reality is the main source of self-created suffering. It emerges from attachment to ideas, feelings, and perceptions about ourselves and others as essential characteristics.

After gaining a little bit of experience in looking at the emptiness of "I"—the "looker," as my student named it—we can begin to investigate the emptiness of what or whom we're looking at, the object of awareness. The process is perhaps best achieved by examining our experience with the intent to recognize the division of each moment of awareness into a looker or a "watcher" and what the looker or watcher perceives is an essentially conceptual invention.

The Buddha often discussed this division of perception in terms of a dream. In a dream, you have a perception of "self" and a perception of "other." Most of his examples were relevant, of course, to the conditions common to the people in the time during which he lived: being attacked by lions and tigers, for instance. I suspect that's not a concern for most of us nowadays—although I've heard from many people about dreams of being chased by monsters or being lost in a big house or landscape.

A more contemporary example might be a dream in which someone gives you a nice, expensive watch: a Rolex, maybe, which I've heard is a very nice, very expensive watch indeed. In the dream you may be thrilled to receive a Rolex without having to pay a single "dream dollar" for it. You may try to show it off, scratching the wrist on which you're wearing it while talking to someone in the dream or pointing out something to someone in a way that reveals your watch.

But then maybe a thief approaches you, slashes your wrist, and steals the Rolex. The pain you experience would feel very real in the dream and your sorrow over losing the watch may be quite intense. You have no dream "insurance" to replace the watch and you're bleeding. You may wake up from the dream sweating or crying, because it all seemed so intense, so real.

But the Rolex was just a dream, wasn't it? And the joy, pain, and grief you experience were all part of the dream. In the context of the dream, they *appeared* real. But when you woke up from the dream, you didn't have a Rolex, there was no thief, and your hand or wrist hadn't been cut. Rolex, thief, wounds, and so on, occurred as expressions of your mind's inherent emptiness and clarity.

In a similar way, whatever we experience in terms of relative reality can be compared to the experiences we undergo in a dream: so vivid, so real, but ultimately reflections of the union of emptiness and clarity.

We can "wake up," so to speak, inside the dream of relative reality and recognize that whatever we experience is the union of emptiness and clarity. Insight practice offers us the opportunity to recognize, on an experiential level, how deeply our perceptions condition our experience. In other words, who and what we perceive is in large part a fabrication of the mind.

Just as when employing insight practice regarding "I," begin by assuming a physical posture that is relaxed and alert. Take a few moments to rest in objectless attention. Next, rest your attention lightly on an object: a visual form, a sound, or a physical sensation. Nice, yes? Very relaxing.

But where is that visual form, that sound, or that physical sensation actually occurring? Somewhere inside the brain? Somewhere "out there"—beyond the body?

Rather than *analyze* where they occur, just look at them (or listen or feel them) as if they were reflections in the mirror of the mind. The object of awareness, the awareness of the object, and the one who is aware of the object all occur simultaneously—just like looking in an ordinary mirror. Without the mirror there would be nothing to be seen, and without the seer there would be no one to see. Joined together, they make seeing possible.

Insight practice offers a way of relating to experience that involves turning the mind inward to look at the mind that is experiencing. This process may be difficult to understand until you try it for yourself. It takes some practice, of course, and the recognition of mind arising simultaneously with experience—the sense of "bigness" described by the student who was going through a divorce—may last only a second or two in the beginning. The temptation in such cases is to say to oneself, "I've got it! I really understand emptiness! Now I can get on with my life in total freedom."

The temptation is particularly strong when working with thoughts and emotions, as well as the way we relate to others and to various situations. The brief glimpses of insight can harden into concepts that can lead us into paths of perception or behavior that may be harmful to ourselves and others. There's an old, old story about a man who spent many years in a cave meditating on emptiness. Inside his cave there were many mice. One day, a rather large mouse jumped up on the stone that served as his table. "Aha," he thought, "the mouse is emptiness." And he grabbed his shoe and killed the mouse, thinking, "The mouse is emptiness, my shoe is emptiness, and killing the mouse is emptiness." But all he'd really done was solidify the idea of emptiness into a concept that nothing exists, so he could do whatever he wanted and feel whatever he felt without experiencing any consequences.

When we turn the mind to look at the mind—whether we're looking for "me," "other," thoughts, or feelings—we can begin, very slowly, to see the mind itself. We become open to the possibility that the mind—the union of emptiness and clarity—is capable of reflecting anything. We're not stuck seeing one thing, but are capable of seeing many possibilities.

9

EMPATHY

A human being is part of a whole called by us the universe.

> —ALBERT EINSTEIN,
> from a letter quoted by Howard Eves,
> *Mathematical Circles Adieu*

THE PEOPLE AROUND us, the situations we face, and the messages from our own senses indicate that who and how we are, are not only subject to change, but can be defined in many different ways that are themselves subject to change. *I am a mother or father. I am a husband or wife. I'm an employee who performs certain tasks in relation to the demands of my employer and other people I work with.*

Nevertheless, deeply entrenched in our habits of relating to ourselves, other people, things, and situations is a kind of lonely separateness—a sense of independent being that obscures our connectedness to others. This very subtle sense of difference or separation lies at the heart of many personal and interpersonal problems. The practice of empathy takes whatever difficulty or crisis we may be facing as a starting point for recognizing our similarity to others. It gradually opens our minds to a profound experience of fearlessness and confidence while transforming personal problems into a strong motivation to help others.

There's an old story, told in several *sutras,* about a woman who had suffered the death of her young son. She refused to believe that her son was dead, however, and ran from house to house in the village asking for medicine to revive her child. Of course, no one could help her. The boy was dead, they pointed out, trying to help her accept the situation. One person, however, recognizing that her mind was deranged by grief, advised her to seek the Buddha—the most capable of physicians—who was staying in a monastery nearby.

Grasping her child closely to her chest, she ran to where the Buddha was staying and asked him for medicine to help her child. The Buddha was in the middle of giving a talk in front of a large number of people; but the woman pushed through, and seeing her distress, the Buddha answered her request. "Go back to your village," he advised, "and bring me back a few mustard seeds from a house where no one has ever died."

She ran back to her village and began asking each of her neighbors for mustard seeds. Her neighbors were happy to give them to her, but then she had to ask, "Has anyone died here?"

They looked at her strangely. Some of them just nodded; others told her yes; and others, perhaps, told her when and under what circumstances a family member's death had occurred.

By the time she completed her circuit of the village, she came to understand through an experience that cut deeper than words that she was not the only person in the world who had suffered a terrible personal loss. Change, loss, and grief were common to all.

Though still grief stricken by the death of her son, she recognized that she was not alone and her heart cracked open. After the funeral ceremonies for her son were completed, she joined the Buddha and the disciples around him. She devoted her life to assisting others in achieving the same degree of recognition.

THE HAPPINESS HANDBOOK

When compassion develops we see that all life is the same,
and that every single being wishes to be happy.

> —Kalu Rinpoche, *The Dharma That Illuminates All Beings*
> *Impartially Like the Light of the Sun and the Moon,*
> translated by Janet Gyatso

It's so easy to think that we're the only ones who suffer while other people were born with the Happiness Handbook alluded to earlier—which, through some accident of birth, we never received. I've been as guilty of this belief as anyone else. When I was young, the anxiety I almost constantly experienced left me feeling alone, weak, and stupid. When I began to practice loving-kindness/compassion, however, I found that my sense of isolation began to diminish. At the same time I gradually began to feel confident and even *useful*. I began to recognize that I wasn't the only person to feel scared and vulnerable. Over time, I began to see that considering the welfare of other beings was essential in discovering my own peace of mind.

Once we've begun to stabilize the mind somewhat through bare attention to our experience, we can begin to proceed to open our attention a little bit more broadly. We can dissolve the delusion of independently existing selves and others through what is known in the Buddhist tradition as loving-kindness/compassion practice. In modern terms, the practice may be better understood as empathy: the ability to identify with or understand the situations in which others may find themselves.

Many people have asked why the practice of empathy is called loving-kindness/compassion. Why not one or the other?

According to the Buddhist understanding, there are two aspects to empathy. *Loving-kindness* refers to the desire for everyone to achieve happiness in this life and the effort we put forth to achieve that goal. *Compassion* is the aspiration to relieve everyone from the fundamental pain and suffering that stems from not knowing their basic nature—and the effort we put forth toward helping them achieve relief from that fundamental pain.

These two concerns, the longing for happiness and the wish to be released from suffering, are common to all living creatures, though not necessarily verbally or consciously, and not always in the complex terms of human consciousness. Suffering and the causes and conditions thereof have been discussed in great detail earlier on. Happiness is a much more generalized term, which may, at its simplest, be described as "flourishing." It means having enough to eat, a place to live, and to go about one's life without threat of harm. Even ants, which I understand don't have a physiological structure that registers pain, still go about their daily tasks of collecting food, bringing it back to the nest, and fulfilling other functions that contribute to their own survival and the survival of their colony.

For most of us the process of developing loving-kindness/compassion develops, as I was taught, in stages. It begins—as with the woman who lost her child—with acknowledging our own suffering and our own wish for release. Gradually, we extend the wish for happiness and the aspiration from release from ourselves to others. This slow and steady path leads from awareness of our own difficulties to an awakening of a potential far deeper and more profound than we could ever imagine as we sit in our cars in the middle of a traffic jam cursing the conditions that caused the delay or standing in line at the bank wishing desperately that the line would move faster.

The initial stage is commonly referred to as *ordinary loving-kindness/compassion,* which begins with developing a sense of loving-kindness and compassion toward oneself and extending it toward those we know. The second stage is often known as *immeasurable loving-kindness/compassion,* an extension of the aspiration for happiness and release from suffering toward those we don't know. The third stage is known as *bodhicitta,* the mind that is awake to the suffering of all sentient beings and spontaneously works to relieve that suffering.

Ordinary Loving-Kindness/Compassion: Focusing on Ourselves

Ordinary loving-kindness/compassion includes several phases. The first involves learning to develop a sense of tenderness toward oneself and an appreciation for one's own positive qualities. It doesn't mean feeling sorry for oneself. It doesn't mean endlessly replaying scenarios of suffering or regrets and thinking about how differently things may have turned out if one or another circumstance had been different. Rather, it involves looking at your experience of yourself in the present moment as an object of meditative focus. In this case, we're not looking for the concept of "I," but rather for the experience of being alive in this moment. If I were to achieve happiness and the causes of happiness, that would be very nice.

Perhaps the simplest method is a kind of variation on the "scanning practice" described in relation to the *shamatha* practice of attention to physical sensations.

Begin by "taming your horse." If you're practicing formally, assume the seven-point posture to the best of your ability. Otherwise, just straighten your spine while keeping the rest of your body relaxed and balanced. "Tame the rider" by allowing your mind simply to relax in a state of objectless attention.

After a few moments, perform a quick "scanning exercise." This time, however, instead of focusing on the sensations themselves, gently allow yourself to recognize that you *have* a body, as well as a mind that's capable of scanning it. Allow yourself to recognize how wonderful these very basic facts of your existence really are and how precious it is to have a body and a mind capable of being aware of the body. Appreciating these gifts plants the seeds for happiness and relief from suffering. There is such relief in simply knowing you're alive and aware.

Rest in that simple appreciation for a moment, and then gently introduce the thought, "How nice it would be if I were always able to enjoy this sense of basic aliveness. How nice it would be if I could always enjoy this sense of well-being and all the causes that lead to feeling contented, open to all possibilities." The words you choose may vary according to your own temperament, of course. In traditional Buddhist terms these thoughts are expressed as a prayer or aspiration: "May I achieve happiness and the causes of happiness. May I be free of suffering and the causes of suffering." But the meaning is essentially the same. Choose the words that work for you.

Then just allow your mind to rest, open and relaxed.

Don't try to maintain this practice for more than a couple of minutes if you're practicing formally or for more than a few seconds if you're practicing informally. You can marvel at being alive and aware just walking through the grocery store, finding yourself caught in a traffic jam, or in the midst of washing dishes. It's very important to practice in short sessions and then allow your mind to rest—otherwise this preciousness can become a concept rather than an experience. Over time, as you gradually repeat the exercise, a realm of possibility begins to open up.

Ordinary Loving-Kindness/Compassion: Focusing on Those Close to Us

Once you've become somewhat familiar with your own experience of relief you can extend that possibility to others. In fact, recognizing the suffering of others can transform your own experience. A friend of mine from Nepal moved to New York City in hopes of finding a better job and earning more money. In Nepal, he'd held a high position in a carpet weaving factory. But upon arriving in New York, the best job he could find was working in a garage—a humiliating comedown from his old job in Nepal. Sometimes, he'd be so upset that he'd start to cry, until one of his managers told him, "What are you doing crying? You can't do that! What would our customers think?"

One day, he noticed someone new working around the garage— a man in a big hat. Taking a closer look, he realized that the man in the hat was the *owner* of the carpet factory in Nepal. He'd given up his business and traveled to New York in the same hopes of earning more money, but he ended up in the same position working as an unskilled laborer in a job that paid less than what he'd made back in Nepal.

All at once, he recognized that he wasn't the only person who had experienced a reversal of fortune. He was not alone.

This is the second stage of ordinary loving-kindness/compassion: acknowledging that whatever is going on inside someone else's mind is probably very similar to what's going on in yours. When we remember this, we gradually come to realize that there's no reason to be frightened of anyone or anything. We're frightened, in most cases, because we don't recognize that whomever or whatever we're facing is just like us: a creature that only wants to flourish.

The classic Buddhist texts teach that we should focus first on our mothers, who have shown the ultimate kindness toward us by carrying us in their bodies and bringing us into the world. Most cultures, Eastern and Western, have traditionally encouraged respect, if not affection, toward one's mother and father both, in return for the sacrifices they've made on our behalf. But this traditional approach has changed a great deal over the past couple of generations. Quite a number of people I've spoken with in recent years don't necessarily enjoy tender and affectionate relationships with their parents, especially in cases where parents have been verbally or physically abusive. In such cases, using one's mother or father as an object of loving-kindness/compassion practice wouldn't be very useful. It's perfectly okay to focus on another object: a kind relative, a supportive teacher, a close friend, spouse, partner, or child. Some people choose to focus on their cats, dogs, or other pets. The object of your meditation doesn't really matter. The important thing is to rest your attention lightly on someone or something toward which you feel a bond of warmth or tenderness.

The practice of ordinary loving-kindness/compassion toward others differs little from the practice of loving-kindness/compassion toward oneself. Begin by assuming either the seven-point posture or at the very least straightening your spine while allowing the rest of your body to rest naturally.

Now, rest for a few moments in objectless attention. Relax in your seat as you would after accomplishing a big task and just observe your mind and all the thoughts, feelings, and sensations passing through it.

After resting a few moments lightly bring your attention to someone or something toward whom you feel some tenderness, affection, or concern. Don't be surprised if the image of someone or something you didn't deliberately choose appears more strongly than the object you may have decided to work with. This happens, often quite spontaneously. One of my students began formal practice intending to focus on his aunt, who had been very kind to him when he was young; but the image that kept appearing to him was a puppy he'd owned as a child. This is just an example of the mind's natural wisdom asserting itself. He actually had a lot of warm memories associated with the puppy, and when he finally surrendered to his memories of the puppy, rather than trying to focus on his aunt, his practice became quite easy.

Allow the sense of warmth or affection to settle in your mind, alternating for a few minutes between these feelings and allowing your mind to simply rest in objectless attention. As you alternate between these two states, allow yourself to wish that the object of your meditation might experience the same sense of openness and warmth you feel toward him or her. After a few moments of alternating between objectless attention and attention to the object of your meditation, you can proceed in a couple of ways. One way is to imagine the object you've chosen in a very sad or painful state. Of course, if the object you've chosen is already in deep pain or sorrow, you can simply bring to mind his or her present condition. Either way, the image you call to mind naturally produces a profound sense of tenderness and connection, and a deep desire to relieve the pain.

Another approach is to rest your attention lightly on whomever or whatever you've chosen while asking yourself, "How much do *I* want to be happy? How much do *I* want to avoid pain or suffering?" Let your thoughts on these points be as specific as possible. For example, if you're stuck somewhere very hot, would you rather move to a cooler and more open place? If you feel some sort of physical pain, would you like the pain to be lifted? As you think about your own answers, gradually turn your attention to the object you've chosen and imagine how he or she would feel in the same situation.

Practicing in this way not only opens your heart to other beings, but also dissolves your own identification with whatever pain or discomfort you may be experiencing at the moment. As my friend from Nepal discovered seeing his former boss working in the same garage in New York, hiding his face under a big hat, we're not alone. People, puppies, and other creatures may seek to flourish and to avoid pain in their own ways, but their basic motivations are quite similar.

Ordinary Loving-Kindness/Compassion: Focusing on Who or What We Don't Like

Cultivating loving-kindness and compassion toward those you know and care about already isn't so hard because even when you want to strangle them for being stupid or obstinate, the bottom line is that you still love them. It's a little bit harder to extend the same sense of warmth and relatedness toward people with whom you may be having personal or professional problems, or toward those whom, for some other reason, you actively dislike.

One student of mine, for example, had a terrible fear of spiders. He dreaded seeing a spider in a corner of a room, or on a windowsill, or worse, according to him, above his bathtub. The spider was just doing what it was doing, spinning a web, hoping to attract a fly or other insect (which probably also had some fear of the spider), but the student would try to anxiously get rid of it, smashing it with a broom or sweeping it up in a vacuum cleaner. After a few months of looking at his own desire to flourish and his own fear of pain and suffering, he began to develop a somewhat different relationship to spiders. Tentatively, he began to approach each encounter differently. Instead of smashing the spider or sweeping it up in a vacuum cleaner, he gathered the courage to capture the spider in a jar and release it outside. Eventually, he even began to say, "Good-bye, little friend. Find your food, find your happiness . . . just not in my house, okay?"

Of course, that didn't stop spiders from showing up in his windows or bathtub, but instead of treating them like enemies he began to recognize them as creatures very much like himself.

Now, capturing spiders in a jar and letting them loose outside may not be a typical route toward developing the second level of ordinary loving-kindness/compassion. But it's a start.

As an exercise, imagine piercing your cheeks with two very sharp needles, one in the left cheek and one in the right. Is the pain you experience in the right cheek any different from the pain you experience in the left? The pain in your right cheek represents the unhappiness and suffering you experience. The pain in the left cheek represents the pain and unhappiness experienced by someone or something you don't like. Is one less painful than the other?

Maybe yes, maybe no. Maybe you've become so used to the needle stuck in the right cheek for so long that you don't notice it much anymore—it's a dull pain. But the needle stuck in your left check is a fresh pain—you're acutely aware of it. You could pull the needle from your right check by working with practicing loving-kindness/compassion with yourself or those toward whom you already feel some tenderness. But the needle in your left cheek remains stuck until you actually begin to extend that aspiration for happiness and relief from suffering to those you don't like. You want them to suffer or to be unhappy. Maybe you feel a jealousy toward them or resentment. But who is feeling the pain of this resentment, jealousy, or dislike?

You.

There's an additional benefit to approaching people you dislike with loving-kindness and compassion. Suppose that person is treating you or someone else unkindly. Now you could approach that person angrily or defensively or even—if your own mood is fairly stable—through reason. But loving-kindness/compassion provides a bit of insight into *why* that person may be saying or doing things that hurt other people. That person is in pain, confused, and is desperately seeking a sense of comfort and stability.

For example, one student of mine had just begun working in the marketing department of a large manufacturing firm and was called into a meeting with a woman who was the head of the accounting department. The meeting started out very badly. The woman was very argumentative, talked nonstop, and if anyone interrupted her or proposed a different point of view, she would grow red in the face and assert her point of view even more strongly.

Sitting back and watching this, my student began looking at the woman with loving-kindness and compassion, and he began to see behind the wall of anger a little girl who had never been listened to as a child. So he began nodding and agreeing with the woman, telling her how intelligent her observations were and what good ideas she had. Slowly, the woman began to relax. Her anger melted and she was able to listen to other people's ideas and actually consider them. My student and the woman didn't become best friends, but after that initial meeting he was almost always invited to meetings with her and always seemed to be able to calm her down; and whenever he had to go to the accounting office, there was a certain sigh of relief from all the other members of the department. His effect was so soothing that the woman would treat the other people in the department a little more kindly.

So it ended up as a "win-win situation" for everybody. Being listened to and appreciated for her intelligence, the woman experienced a bit of relief from her own suffering. The people who worked under her weren't subject to constant criticism, so the unpleasant feelings they experienced toward her also began to loosen.

And my student began to experience more confidence in himself as he began to see that he could handle difficult situations with the clarity and wisdom born of loving-kindness/compassion.

Immeasurable Loving-Kindness/Compassion
Of course, developing loving-kindness and compassion toward those we know already isn't so hard after a bit of practice. It's a little bit more of a stretch to extend the same sense of warmth and relatedness toward those we don't know, and in many cases, can't even possibly know. As we hear about tragedies around the world, or even in our neighborhoods, a sense of helplessness and hopelessness may develop. There are only so many causes we can join,

and sometimes our work and family lives prevent us from helping out in a direct way. The practice of immeasurable loving-kindness/compassion helps to relieve that sense of hopelessness. It also fosters a sense of confidence that whatever situation in which we find ourselves and whomever we face, we have a basis for relating in a way that is not quite so fearful or hopeless. We can see possibilities to which we might otherwise be blind and begin to develop a greater appreciation for the possibilities within us.

A particularly useful practice for generating immeasurable loving-kindness/compassion is known in Tibetan as *tonglen*, which may be translated into English as "sending and taking." *Tonglen* is actually quite a simple practice, requiring only a simple coordination of visualization and breathing.

The first step, as always, is to find a restful position for your body and then to rest your mind in objectless attention. Then gently bring your attention to this thought: "Just as I want to achieve happiness and avoid suffering, other beings also feel the same way." You don't need to visualize specific beings, although you may start out with a specific visualization if you find it helpful. Eventually, though, *tonglen* extends beyond anyone or anything you can imagine to include animals, insects, and all the creatures who have suffered or will suffer in any way.

The point, as I was taught, is simply to remember that the world is filled with an infinite number of beings, and to think: *Just as I want happiness, all beings want happiness. Just as I wish to avoid suffering, all beings wish to avoid suffering.* Just as you worked with ordinary loving-kindness/compassion, as you allow these thoughts to roll around in your mind you'll actually begin to find yourself actively engaged in wishing for others' happiness and freedom from suffering.

The next step is to focus on your breathing as a means of sending whatever happiness you may have experienced or are currently experiencing to all sentient beings and absorb their suffering. As you exhale, imagine all the happiness and benefits you've acquired during your life pouring out of yourself in the form of clear light. This light extends out toward all beings and dissolves into them, fulfilling all their needs and eliminating their suffering. As you inhale, imagine the pain and suffering of all sentient beings as a dark, oily smoke being absorbed through your nostrils and dissolving into your heart. As you continue this practice, imagine that all beings are freed from suffering and filled with bliss and happiness.

After practicing in this way for a few moments, simply allow your mind to rest. Then take up the practice again, alternating between periods of *tonglen* and resting your mind.

If it helps your visualization, you can sit with your body very straight and rest your hands in loosely closed fists on the tops of your thighs. As you breathe out, open your fingers and slide your hands down your thighs toward your knees while you imagine the light going out toward all beings. As you inhale, slide your hands back up, forming loosely closed fists as though drawing the dark light of others' suffering and dissolving it into yourself.

The world is filled with so many different kinds of creatures, it's impossible even to imagine them all, much less offer direct and immediate help to each and every one. But through the practice of *tonglen,* you open your mind to infinite creatures and wish for their well-being. The result is that eventually your mind becomes clearer, calmer, and more focused and aware. You develop the capacity to help others in infinite ways, both directly and indirectly.

Bodhicitta

The final stage is *bodhicitta*, a Sanskrit term often translated as the "mind of awakening" or "awakened mind." It's a compound word that combines the Sanskrit term *bodhi* (which comes from the Sanskrit root verb *budh*, which translates as "to become awake, to become aware, to notice, or to understand") and the word *citta* (which is usually translated as "mind" or sometimes as "spirit" in the sense of "inspiration").

Within the Buddhist tradition, we recognize two kinds of *bodhicitta*: absolute and relative. *Absolute bodhicitta* refers to the mind that has become completely pure through accomplishing all the levels of training and which, consequently, sees the nature of reality directly, without question or wavering. The seed of buddha nature latent within all sentient beings has grown into a magnificent tree. Capable of seeing and knowing everything, *absolute bodhicitta* includes an acute awareness of the suffering all creatures endure when they are ignorant of their own nature. It also includes a longing to release all beings from that deepest level of suffering. This is the state the Buddha attained, as well as those who followed in his footsteps to attain complete enlightenment.

Few among us are capable of experiencing *absolute bodhicitta* right away, however. In his own lifetime, the historical Buddha worked for six years to arrive at this fully awakened awareness. According to legend, he was only able to accomplish this in such a relatively short period because he'd spent many, many lifetimes working toward this goal.

Most of us need to train along the more gradual path of *relative bodhicitta*. This extends the various loving-kindness/compassion practices a bit further in terms of the cultivation of the desire for all sentient beings to realize—not in an intellectual sense, but through actual experience—the full blossoming of their buddha nature and taking the actions to accomplish that goal.

Developing relative *bodhicitta* always involves two aspects: aspiration and application. *Aspiration bodhicitta* involves cultivating the heartfelt desire to raise all sentient beings to the level at which they completely recognize their true nature. We begin by thinking, "I wish to attain complete awakening in order to help all sentient beings attain the same state." Most Buddhist practices begin with some sort of prayer expressing this aspiration. Simply reciting this prayer, in whatever language or whatever terms you're familiar with, is of course very helpful in that it helps us to broaden the goal of our practice. But such prayers and aspirations remain simply words until we actually spend some time working with ordinary and immeasurable states of loving-kindness/compassion. As we've seen earlier, there's no way we can experience complete happiness and an end to suffering for ourselves without direct experience of our own and others' desire for happiness and release from suffering. Working toward our own release is like pulling the needle only out of one cheek. As long as a needle remains in our other cheek, we'll always feel a bit of discomfort, pain, or fear.

Sounds like a big job, doesn't it? It seems hard enough to awaken ourselves, much less bring others to the same awakening. But if we look back at the story of the woman who had lost her child, we can begin to sense that in the presence of someone who is awake, it becomes possible for other people to become awake as well. Sometimes this awakening may take the form of following advice, listening to a teaching, or following the example of a teacher.

Application bodhicitta focuses on the path of attaining the goal of awakening other people. Aspiration is the desire to carry people from one "place" to another. Application is the means by which we carry out our aspiration.

There are many ways to practice application *bodhicitta*. For example, refraining from stealing, lying, gossiping, and speaking or acting in ways that intentionally cause pain. Also, acting generously toward others, patching up quarrels, speaking gently and calmly rather than "flying off the handle," and rejoicing in the good things that happen to other people rather than allowing ourselves to become overwhelmed by jealousy or envy.

Conduct of this sort extends the experience of loving-kindness/compassion in meditation into every aspect of daily life. This creates a win-win situation for everybody. *We* win because we recognize that we're not alone in experiencing difficult emotions or problematic situations. As this recognition sinks in, we begin to feel a deeper sense of confidence in ourselves and are able to respond more thoughtfully and compassionately to others. Those around us win because, having developed an intuitive sense of their suffering, we begin to act toward them in kinder, more considerate ways. And they, in turn, begin to behave more compassionately toward others.

There is no greater inspiration and no greater courage than the intention to lead all beings to the perfect freedom and complete well-being of recognizing their true nature. Whether you accomplish the goal isn't important. The intention alone has such power that as you work with it, your mind will become stronger, your mental and emotional habits will diminish, and you'll become more skillful in helping other beings. In so doing, you'll create the causes and conditions for your own well-being.

The understanding of suffering and its causes, the potential inherent within us, and the means of transforming that understanding into experience could be regarded as the Happiness Handbook we thought we'd missed at birth.

But, as many people have asked, how do we apply the lessons of understanding and experience to our own situations? What do we do when faced with anxiety, grief, jealousy, anger, or despair?

To answer these questions we have to explore a little more deeply, using our own lives as a laboratory of experience.

PART THREE

APPLICATION

The seed contained in the fruit of a mango or similar trees [is possessed of] the indestructible property of sprouting.

—*The Mahayana Uttaratantra Shastra,*
translated by Rosemarie Fuchs

10

LIFE ON THE PATH

Everything can be used as an invitation to meditation.

—SOGYAL RINPOCHE,
The Tibetan Book of Living and Dying
edited by Patrick Gaffney and Andrew Harvey

TO CUT THROUGH problems, we need problems.

That may sound a bit strange, even radical. But in his day, the Buddha was a radical who proposed a treatment plan for suffering that differed in many ways from the options offered by some of his contemporaries.

I remember as a child hearing about a tradition among hermit meditators in Tibet—men and women who spent months and often years in isolated mountain caves where they could practice for long periods without distraction. Sounds nice, doesn't it? A simple life without disturbances and a perfect situation in which to develop peace of mind—except for one small detail.

It was too peaceful.

Living alone in a mountain cave doesn't present many opportunities to grapple with disturbing thoughts, emotions, or other forms of *dukkha*. So every once in a while, these hermit meditators would come down from the mountains, enter a town or village, and start saying or doing crazy things. The townspeople or villagers would get so angry that they would shout at them, hurl insults at them, or even physically beat them. But for the meditators the verbal, emotional, and physical abuse they suffered became supports for meditation. They became opportunities to develop greater mental and emotional stability and to cut ever more deeply through layers of misperception about their own nature, the nature of others, and the nature of their experience.

As their understanding grew, their recognition of the basic situation of suffering and its causes deepened and they developed a more acute awareness of the confusion that rules the lives of so many people: the self-created suffering rooted in a belief in permanence, independence, and singularity. Their hearts broke for these people, opening a deep and personal experience of lovingkindness and compassion. They would sit for hours, using some of the practices described earlier, to send the benefits they'd gained to the people who'd helped them grow by taunting and beating them.

Most of us aren't hermit meditators, of course, and in this respect we're actually very lucky. We don't have to go looking for problems or make appointments to meet with them. We don't have to pay a cent for disturbing thoughts and emotions. Our lives are bounded by challenges of every conceivable variety.

How do we deal with them?

Typically we try either to deny or to eliminate them—treating them as enemies—or allow them to overwhelm us, treating them as "bosses."

A third option—the middle way exemplified by the hermit meditators of old—is to use our experiences as a means of opening to a deeper realization of our capacity for wisdom, kindness, and compassion.

In Buddhist terms, this approach is often referred to as "taking your life on the path."

Your life, exactly as it is—right here, right now.

The radical goal of the Buddha's treatment plan is not to solve or eliminate problems, but to use them as a basis or focus for recognizing our potential. Every thought, every emotion, and every physical sensation is an opportunity to turn our attention inward and become a little bit more familiar with the source.

Many people look at meditation as an exercise, like going to the gym. "I've gotten that over with! Now I can go on with the rest of my life." But meditation isn't something separate from your life. It *is* your life.

In a sense, we're always meditating: focusing on emotional turmoil, disturbing thoughts, and drawing conclusions from our experiences about who and what we are and the nature of our environment. This sort of meditation often occurs spontaneously, without our conscious participation.

Taking our lives on the path raises the process of unconscious meditation to a conscious level. Many people, including myself, embrace this approach in hopes of finding immediate solutions to mental and emotional pain. Of course, it's possible to feel some sort of relief right away, but the experience usually doesn't last very long. It's not uncommon for people to become disappointed when the sense of freedom dissolves and to think "Oh, this Buddhist stuff doesn't work."

But if we continue, beginning by just taking a few moments throughout the day to look at our experience and then perhaps extending our formal practice sessions, we discover that the Buddha's treatment plan is much more than psychological aspirin. As we examine our thoughts, feelings, and sensations, we discover something precious.

HIDDEN GOLD

> *A precious treasure is contained in each being's mind.*
>
> —*The Mahayana Uttaratantra Shastra,*
> translated by Rosemarie Fuchs

There's an old, old story about an Indian man who, crossing a muddy field, accidentally dropped a nugget of gold he was carrying. The field became a convenient place for people in the area to dump their garbage, scraps of food, and so on, which dissolved into a muddy sort of waste. The gold lay there for centuries, covered by increasing mounds of mud and garbage. Finally, a god peered down and spoke to a man who was looking for gold, saying, "Look, there's a huge nugget buried deep under all that junk. Dig it up, make something useful out of it—a piece of jewelry or something—so this precious substance doesn't go to waste."

The story, of course, is an analogy for the recognition of buddha nature, which is often obscured by the "mud" of ignorance, desire, aversion, and the various types of mental and emotional turmoil that spring from these three basic poisons.

The Buddha's original teachings and the commentaries written by later masters provide a lot of analogies to help people understand buddha nature, which in itself is beyond description. But the example of gold seems to be the easiest for people to understand. So when I teach on the subject, one of the first questions I ask is, "What is the quality of gold?"

The answers vary.

"Shiny."

"Untarnishable."

"Durable."

"Precious."

"Rare."

"Expensive!"

"Perfect."

All very reasonable responses.

Then I ask a second question: "Is there any difference between the nugget of gold buried in mud and garbage for centuries and the nugget that has been unearthed and cleansed of mud?"

The answer, invariably, is "No."

Centuries of mud can't change the nature of gold any more than emotional or mental disturbances can alter our essential nature. But just as a thick coat of mud can make a nugget of pure gold *look* like an ordinary lump of rock, so our misperceptions and fixations can conceal our essential nature. We tend to see ourselves, in a sense, as mud-covered rocks.

Like gold hunters scraping away the coats of mud and filth to reveal even one patch of a nugget of pure gold, in order to catch a glimpse of the "golden nugget" of buddha nature, we have to start scraping away at the "mud" that obscures it.

For most of us it is a slow and gradual process. It takes time to adjust to new and possibly uncomfortable ideas about the nature of ourselves and the reality in which we function. It takes time, as well, to cultivate through practice a more attentive and less judg-mental relationship to the myriad forms of self-created suffering that make up the greater part of our experience.

I grew up in a culture steeped in Buddhist philosophy and practice, and was fortunate to benefit from the patient efforts of wise and experienced teachers who had received their own training in an unbroken lineage handed directly from teacher to student stretching all the way back to the Buddha himself. Yet even given such auspicious circumstances, it was hard to comprehend my essential nature as free, clear, capable, and so on. I believed what my father and other teachers said was true, but I just couldn't see it in myself—especially when anxiety and other powerful emotions gripped me so tightly I could hardly breathe.

So it comes as no surprise when people ask, "If I'm supposed to have all these great qualities, why do I feel so terrible? Why am I so angry? Why do I feel so anxious? Or hopeless? Or depressed? Why am I always arguing with my husband (or wife, or child, or friend)?"

BUDDHA NATURE BLOCKERS

What is reborn are our habits.

—His Holiness the Dalai Lama, *The Path to Tranquility*,
compiled and edited by Renuka Singh

There are a number of ways to answer this question.

To begin with, there's a lot of old, dry mud to cut through. Thrust into a realm in which everything changes—second by second, cell by cell, and atom by atom—we long for certainty, stability, and satisfaction. The three basic poisons ignorance, attachment, and aversion could be described as a very basic set of responses to this longing. We engender a generalized point of view grounded in dualistic terms such as self and other and subject and object. We define these distinctions as good or bad and pleasant or unpleasant, and invest them with qualities of permanence, singularity, and independence.

Of course, the habit of organizing and interpreting experience in relative terms doesn't develop overnight. We don't wake up one morning and decide, "Aha, I'm going to start defining my world dualistically!"

As discussed earlier, our physiological constitution—the relationship between our sense organs, the various structures in our brain, and the automatic responses of other physical systems—predisposes us toward organizing our experiences in terms of distinctions. Our cultural and familial backgrounds, as well as the events that occur in our individual lives, meanwhile, nurture and enhance this biological predisposition. Gradually, a kind of cyclical relationship evolves. As perception influences experience, experience influences behavior; behavior reinforces experience, and experience reinforces perception. Layer upon layer of mud accumulates.

The *Abhidharma*—a collection of texts that extends the Buddha's teaching in greater detail on the relationship between perception, experience, and behavior—lists eighty-four thousand different types of mental and emotional afflictions that emerge through various combinations and recombinations of the root habits of ignorance, attachment, and aversion. That's a lot of mud! We could spend our entire lives searching through eighty-four thousand combinations to figure out which of them fit our particular situation.

Some of these combinations form close bonds, however. I've found over the years that many of the challenges we face in life could be more easily understood through exploring how, on a very basic level, these specific combinations affect our views about ourselves, others, our relationships, and the various situations we face on a daily basis. In particular, the *Mahayana Uttaratantra Shastra*, one of the most detailed teachings on buddha nature, offers a short, five-point list of habits of organizing experience that undercut our recognition of our essential nature and underlie much of the mental and emotional turmoil we suffer.

In modern psychological terms, these habits are often referred to as *distortions* or *schemas*, cognitive structures that lock us into a limited and limiting view of ourselves, others, and the world around us. I think of them as "Buddha Nature Blockers." These are habits of organizing and responding to experience that inhibit us from experiencing our lives with a deep awareness of freedom, clarity, wisdom, and wonder that transcends the conventional psychotherapeutic model of simply becoming okay, well-adjusted, or normal.

The Buddha's plan went far beyond learning to become "okay." His aim was for us to become buddhas: to awaken our capacity to approach every experience—grief, shame, jealousy, frustration, illness, and even death—with the innocent perspective we experience when looking for the first time, for example, at the Grand Canyon, Yellowstone National Park, or the views from the top of Taipei 101. Before fear, judgment, anxiety, or opinion intervenes, there's a moment of direct pristine awareness that transcends any distinction between experience and the experiencer.

The Sanskrit and Tibetan description of these combinations, or Buddha Nature Blockers, as described in the *Mahayana Uttaratantra Shastra,* are very long. By way of introduction, I think it's probably best to condense them in a way that may be more easily understood by contemporary audiences.

On a purely literal level, the first Buddha Nature Blocker is known as "fainteartedness" or "timidity." On a deeper level, the term points to a deeply ingrained tendency to judge or to criticize ourselves, exaggerating what we may perceive as defects in thought, feeling, character, or behavior. In our own eyes, we deem ourselves incompetent, insufficient, or "bad."

I remember an incident that occurred during my first teaching tour of North America at the age of twenty-three. My brother, Tsoknyi Rinpoche, had been scheduled to teach, but other obligations prevented him from traveling, so I was sent in his place. Two weeks into the tour, a woman was ushered into a room set aside for private interviews. After preliminary introductions were made, she sat down and, to put her at ease, I asked her a few general questions about how she was getting along in the public teachings, whether she understood what I was trying to say, and if she had any specific questions.

After this initial conversation, she sat silently for a moment. Her whole body became tense. She squeezed her eyes shut, took in a deep breath, exhaled, and opened her eyes.

Then, in a small voice, almost a whisper, she said, "I hate myself."

Looking back on that confession, I realize how much courage it must have taken for her to say those words. In those early days of my North American teaching, I had very little knowledge of the English language and always needed a translator nearby. So the woman who came for a private interview was not only confessing her deepest discomfort to me but also to the translator seated in the room.

Yet even though the translator accurately interpreted her words, I was a bit confused. Among the eighty-four thousand mental and emotional conflicts discussed in the *Abhidharma*, there's undoubtedly one that corresponds to "self-hatred." But the term itself was new to me, so I found myself in the awkward position of asking her what she meant.

She became tense again and then started to cry.

"I can't do anything right. Ever since I can remember, people have told me that I'm clumsy and stupid. My mother scolded me for not setting the table right or cleaning the dishes right. My teachers told me I could never learn. I tried so hard in school and at home to do everything correctly. But the harder I tried, the more I hated myself for being so awkward and stupid. I've got an okay job, but I'm always afraid that someone will point out a mistake, and I get so anxious that I *do* make mistakes. I sing in my church choir, but when people compliment me on my voice, all I can think of is how I didn't hit the note right and that people are only saying nice things because they pity me.

"I feel so helpless, so hopeless. I want to be somebody else. I look at other people around me laughing, going out to lunch or dinner with friends, getting ahead with their lives, and I wonder why can't I be like them? What's wrong with me?"

As I listened, I began to think back to my early childhood: the thoughts, feelings, and often physical sensations of anxiety and panic, as well as the sense of failure that overcame me when I couldn't grasp the lessons my father and other early teachers had offered me. After a few days of looking back on my own experience in this way, I began to catch a glimpse of what self-hatred might feel like. I can't say that I managed to create precisely the same self-critical thoughts and emotions that haunted this woman. *Dukkha* is a universal condition, but the particular form in which it manifests itself varies from individual to individual. The process of examining this woman's distress challenged me to consider what for me seemed a new language of discontent: words, terms, and experiences specific to the lives of people living in different cultures.

In order to assist people in understanding and applying the principles and practices that had been passed down to me from my teachers, I needed to absorb this new language. I had to translate the lessons I'd learned in ways that would be relevant to the issues faced by people living in this new world of personal and cultural expression I'd entered.

Self-hatred is, perhaps, an extreme example of the first Buddha Nature Blocker, the tendency to belittle ourselves. Over the years, I've heard many people express similar sentiments, though in different, sometimes less severe, terms. Some of them were familiar to me: guilt, shame, or anger toward oneself for not completing a goal or saying or doing things in "the heat of the moment."

A number of people I've met with have spoken, too, about feelings of low self-esteem: a nagging doubt over the ability to achieve anything and the more or less constant habit of putting themselves down or seeing very little possibility of succeeding in whatever activity in which they're engaged. I've also heard people speak about performance anxiety, a sense that the work they're doing is just not good enough. They drive themselves harder and harder, becoming perfectionists or "workaholics." The same sort of drive can be seen in such personal behavior as tying ourselves in knots over what we should or shouldn't do in social situations. Some people I've spoken with simply "freeze up" when confronted with situations in which people they know or care for are experiencing physical, emotional, or mental pain. They don't know what to do and are overcome by what one woman described as "an overwhelming sense of awfulness."

Hopelessness, helplessness, despair, and other painful feelings are also closely tied to physical disease. For example, depression is a physiological disorder far different from feeling sad or depressed. From my discussions with experts in the fields of neuroscience and psychology, painful rounds of self-criticism reinforce the potency of the physical disease—which, in turn, enhances the destructive thoughts and feelings that accompany it. Addiction, whether to alcohol, drugs, food, gambling, or other self-destructive behaviors, is another disorder that, according to most of the doctors and psychologists with whom I've spoken, is also biologically rooted. Alcohol or drugs, for example, tend to provide an artificial sense of poise and assurance to people who lack confidence in themselves or their ability to connect with others.

A hurricane of mental, emotional, and physical responses erupts as well when confronted with other forms of natural suffering: the various forms of illness, accident, aging, and, ultimately, death.

Of the five Buddha Nature Blockers, self-judgment is perhaps the easiest to identify. Thoughts and feelings of inadequacy, guilt, shame, and so on, "live" close to the surface of awareness. It's somewhat more difficult for us to recognize our judgmental attitude toward others, which is the essence of the second Blocker. Often translated as "contempt for inferior beings," this second impediment represents the opposite extreme of what we might call the dimension of judgment: a critical view of others. A narrow interpretation of this point of view is that everyone else is less important, less competent, or less deserving than oneself. More broadly, it's a tendency to blame others for the challenges we experience: *Someone else* is always standing in our way, and that someone else is simply wrong, bad, stubborn, ignorant, or manipulative. While self-judgment represents, in a sense, an inability to empathize with ourselves, the opposite end of the spectrum reflects an inability to see anything good in others or to listen to what they have to say.

Sometimes such judgments are obvious. For instance, when two people fall in love, there's an initial period of seeing their partner as completely perfect—the total fulfillment of their dreams. But after a few months, "imperfections" surface. Arguments arise. Disappointment and dissatisfaction grow. Each partner is overtaken by a strong tendency to define the other as "the bad one," the source of irritation and pain. This tendency can become especially painful if a couple is married or have lived together for many years, sharing a home and various financial arrangements.

The same sorts of judgments can arise in professional situations as well. Recently, a student voiced a complaint that someone he was working with was always putting him down, saying nasty things about him, and undermining the position he held in the organization within which they both worked. He was angry and had begun to think of this fellow worker as an enemy, someone out to destroy him. He blamed the other fellow for whatever problems he was having at work, thinking of him as "cruel," "spiteful," and "deliberately destructive."

Sometimes, though, our judgments of others can be expressed in subtler ways. For example, one of my students recently told a story about a woman he knew who was grieving over the death of a close family member. She'd received a condolence call from a friend whose sibling had died recently, so in talking with him she began speaking quite openly about her own grief. During the conversation she began to hear the click of the keys in the background and realized that he was checking and responding to e-mail. She felt, as she described it, "kicked in the stomach." Her friend wasn't really listening. His own interests overrode his capacity to be fully present to the woman's grief, and he wasn't even aware of the devastating effect this disconnection had on his friend or even on himself: not only had he deprived his friend of the compassion she needed at the time, but he had isolated himself as well.

Just as the first and second Buddha Nature Blockers represent extremes of judgment, the third and fourth represent opposing views about the nature of experience, perspectives that could be said to hold the first two distortions in place.

The third could be translated in a variety of ways: "seeing the untrue as true," "holding what is inauthentic as authentic," or, more loosely, "seeing the unreal as real." Basically, all these terms signify an adherence to the belief that the qualities we see in ourselves, others, or conditions are truly, permanently, or inherently existing. In Buddhist terms, this tendency would be known as *eternalism*—a tendency to hold certain aspects of experience as absolute and enduring rather than as a combination of temporary combinations of causes and conditions. Perhaps a simpler means of describing this perspective is "being stuck." We are who we are, others are the way they are, situations are as they are, and that's that.

The fourth, "seeing the true as untrue," represents the reverse perspective: a denial, or perhaps more strongly, a rejection of buddha nature altogether. The idea of fundamentally pure, clear, free nature sounds very nice, but deep in your heart you believe it's pretty much a fantasy—an idea dreamed up by mystics. Whereas you might describe the third as seeing the mud, so to speak, as a permanent, impenetrable coating, the fourth might be explained as seeing that there's *only* mud. This perspective is often understood as *nihilism*: an elementary despair that cannot admit, within oneself or others, the possibility of freedom, wisdom, capabilities, or potential. In more colloquial terms, you might call this a basic "blind spot."

The fifth and final Buddha Nature Blocker, which might be considered the foundation of the others, is traditionally interpreted as self-obsession. In contemporary terms, we can understand it as the "myth of me"—a desperate longing for stability in terms of "me" and "mine." *My* situation, *my* opinion—whether it involves self-judgment, judgment of others, being stuck, or being blind—at least reflects a still point in an ever-turning realm of experience. We cling to our opinions, our storylines, our personal mythologies, with the same desperation with which we hold to the sides of a roller coaster cart.

WORKING RELATIONSHIPS

The shadow of a bird soaring in the sky may be temporarily invisible, but it is still there and will always appear when the bird comes to earth.

—The Treasury of Precious Qualities,
translated by the Padmakara Translation Group

None of the situations we experience is caused solely by one or another of these Buddha Nature Blockers. They work together, like a group of dictators that form an alliance to assert control—not over geographical boundaries but mental and emotional ones. One may play a more dominant role than another, yet each contributes in different ways to the mode in which we think, feel, and act.

For example, a few years ago during one of my teaching tours, I met a married couple who both had well-paying jobs, a comfortable home, two cars, and a couple of TV sets and stereo systems. Over the years, they'd achieved a standard of living that stood in sharp contrast to the conditions I see in other parts of the world.

But one weekend while taking a drive through the countryside they passed through a neighborhood dominated by large houses and acres of rolling lawns and gardens. And they began to wonder, "Why shouldn't we move to a bigger house? Why shouldn't we live in a richer neighborhood? Wouldn't we be happier?"

The idea seemed quite logical at the time, so they bought a big house in a wealthy neighborhood.

Soon after they moved in, they began to see that their neighbors had very expensive cars. Every time their neighbors came out of their houses they were wearing new designer clothes. Their neighbors' friends also dressed in expensive clothes and drove expensive cars. So the couple bought new, expensive cars for themselves and new, expensive clothes. No matter how much they spent, though, they always *felt* like they were competing with their neighbors.

The pressure to maintain a high style of living eventually began to cause problems in the couple's relationship. They had to work longer hours to cover their expenses. They argued over money: how it should be earned, invested, and spent. Eventually the stress became so great that they both lost their jobs and ended up angry and frustrated with each other, bitterly fighting over every little thing.

"What should we do?" they begged during a private interview.

I gave them a little bit of homework.

"What is the source of your difficulty?" I asked. "Is it your house? Your cars? Your clothes? Your neighbors? Take a couple of days to look at your situation and then come back and let me know what you discover."

They had already received some instruction in simply looking at thoughts and emotions without judgment, and I urged them to view their situation in this light: not blaming themselves or others, but simply observing the thoughts and emotions passing through their awareness.

When they came back, it turned out that the problem wasn't the cars, the house, the clothes, or the neighbors.

"I looked at those houses, those people and their cars, and I felt I wanted more than what I had," the husband said.

"I envied them," his wife added. "But they never invited us to their parties. They never even welcomed us to the neighborhood. I started to think, 'They're not very nice people. Snooty people. Well, I'll show them!'"

"And so we bought more things," the husband went on, "bigger cars, expensive clothes." He shrugged. "But it didn't seem to make any impression."

"All that stuff," the wife sighed. "We were happy with it for a while, but . . ."

"And when you started fighting with each other?" I asked.

"Oh, it went back and forth," the wife sighed. "'I was right about this.' 'I was right about that.' 'You were wrong about this.' 'You were wrong about that.' Oh, it just went on for months."

As they laid out each observation, their shoulders relaxed and the tension in their faces, legs, and arms released. They were already beginning to look at their present experience as an accumulation of thoughts and feelings that had built up over years. But what amazed me was the interplay between the Buddha Nature Blockers. These were the ways in which judgments about themselves and others—deep-seated beliefs of permanence, singularity, and independence; a blindness to their inner potential; and attachment to a particular perspective based on how "I" see things as correct and appropriate—acted upon one another.

"So what are you going to do now?" I asked.

They glanced at each other.

"I don't think we're in a position right now to make any big decisions," the wife replied. "I think we have to take some time to look at the way we look."

"Looking at the way we look" is the essence of taking life on the path. Certainly, we're all going to experience changes and challenges in our lives. But if we look at the way we look at them, something quite wonderful begins to happen. The layers of mud that obscure our potential become fertile soil, in which the seeds of wisdom, loving-kindness, and compassion begin to stir, take root, and sprout. The Buddha Nature Blockers become buddha nature "breakthroughs."

How?

Through applying the understanding of our basic situation together with the practices of attention, insight, and empathy.

11

MAKING IT PERSONAL

When you are face to face with a difficulty, you are up against a discovery.

—William Thompson, Lord Kelvin, *Baltimore Lectures*

I OFTEN TEACH in group settings. So when I explain how to work with thoughts and emotions using the three methods described in Part Two, I tend to use simple examples that most people can relate to, such as anger, fear, or—sometimes drawing on my own experience—anxiety. Almost invariably, however, someone will ask, "Okay, I understand how to work with anger and fear, but how do I work with jealousy?" Someone else may ask for an explanation about working with depression or loneliness or low self-esteem.

Actually, the same methods can be used to work with any emotional or mental state. It's not as though one method is specifically appropriate for anger, another for grief, another for anxiety, and so on. If that were the case, we'd need eighty-four thousand different methods to work with each possible mental or emotional conflict!

Even that many methods might not be sufficient, since no two individuals' experiences are exactly the same. For some people, a particular state dominates their lives over long periods. Feelings of depression, isolation, guilt, or fear of failure are vividly present and seemingly inescapable. For others, thoughts and emotions are more varied. Jealousy, sadness, anger, and so on, may linger for a while, alternating with periods of feeling relaxed and content.

Still others may not be at all clear about what they're feeling. As a student of mine recently confessed, "For a long time it seemed as though I was just moving day to day through a kind of fog or cloud. I was functioning—going to work, buying groceries, paying bills, and so forth—but I didn't really feel involved in anything I was doing. There were no real highs, no real lows. Inside, I was more or less blank, doing things because they were what I was supposed to do."

Another type of fog can envelop us when we encounter an unexpected, acutely unpleasant situation. For example, a Taiwanese woman I met a while back told me about a terrible shock she'd received years earlier, when her husband announced that he was going to China on a business trip. A few days after he left, she decided that she would take some time for herself and visit a resort in the south of Taiwan. As she was entering a restaurant, she saw her husband with another woman. "I was stunned," she said. "For the first few minutes I didn't know what to think or what to feel. And then all of a sudden, I had too many feelings. I was furious, hurt, and jealous. I felt betrayed and foolish. I wanted to run over and confront them and I wanted to just disappear into the ground. It took months to sort out all those feelings, and I still don't think I'm finished yet. Sometimes, they all come flooding back, and sometimes I find myself reliving that first moment of being absolutely numb."

As I've listened to people describe their particular situations or ask for methods to deal with specific emotions, I've come to realize that it would be more useful to present the three practices of attention, insight, and empathy in terms of step-by-step processes that can be applied to any mental or emotional state. The steps themselves are simple and consistent across each of the three practices.

There are several benefits to adopting this step-by-step approach. The first involves a practical method of relieving the immediate conditions of mental and emotional pain. The second is to draw attention to the influence of deep-seated beliefs—the Buddha Nature Blockers—that hold certain mental and emotional patterns in place. The third, and most significant, benefit involves recognizing the Buddha Nature Blockers as creations of the mind. As we begin to recognize the mind's power to influence our experience, we can begin to work with that power and discover within ourselves a freedom previously unimagined. To put it simply, when we take the time to look at the way we see things, the way we see things changes.

Over the next few pages, we'll examine the steps in detail. For the moment, they can be summarized as follows: The Main Exercise, Try Something Different, Step Back, and Take a Break.

Let's start by examining how to apply these steps in the context of *shamatha*, the most basic of the three practices, and the most important for anyone setting out on the path of meditation.

THE AIM OF ATTENTION

Self-awareness . . . is a neutral mode that maintains self-reflectiveness even in the midst of turbulent emotions.
—Daniel Goleman, *Emotional Intelligence*

Ordinarily, our minds are like flags in the wind, fluttering this way and that, depending on which way the wind blows. Even if we don't want to feel angry, jealous, lonely, or depressed, we're carried away by such feelings and by the thoughts and physical sensations that accompany them. We're not free; we can't see other options, other possibilities.

The goal of attention, or *shamatha,* practice is to become aware of awareness. Awareness is the basis, or what you might call the "support," of the mind. It is steady and unchanging, like the pole to which the flag of ordinary consciousness is attached. When we recognize and become grounded in awareness of awareness, the "wind" of emotion may still blow. But instead of being carried away by the wind, we turn our attention inward, watching the shifts and changes with the intention of becoming familiar with that aspect of consciousness which recognizes *Oh, this is what I'm feeling, this is what I'm thinking.* As we do so, a bit of space opens up within us. With practice, that space—which is the mind's natural clarity—begins to expand and settle. We can begin to watch our thoughts and emotions without necessarily being affected by them quite as powerfully or vividly as we're used to. We can still feel our feelings, think our thoughts, but slowly our identity shifts from a person who defines him- or herself as lonely, ashamed, frightened, or hobbled by low self-esteem to a person who can look at loneliness, shame, and low self-esteem as movements of the mind.

It's not unusual, especially in the beginning, to worry, *Am I aware of awareness and at the same time aware of thoughts and emotions?* Actually, there's no need to worry. Once you've received the instructions, you know that the goal of practice is simply to develop awareness. Once you recognize your goal, awareness of awareness begins to grow and stabilize naturally.

The process is not unlike going to the gym. You have a goal—whether it's losing weight, building muscles, promoting your health, or some other reason. In order to achieve that goal, you lift weights, jog on a treadmill, take classes, and so on. Gradually, you begin to see the fruits of these activities; and seeing them, you're inspired to continue.

In the case of attention practice, the important point is to know that the goal is to establish and develop stability of awareness that will allow you to look at thoughts, emotions, and even physical pain without wavering. Bearing that in mind, let's look at applying the steps.

Step One: The Main Exercise

The main exercise of attention practice can be broken down into three stages. The first involves simply looking at a thought or emotion with what, in Buddhist terms, is known as *ordinary awareness*—bringing attention to thoughts or feelings without any express purpose or intention. Just notice and identify what you're thinking or feeling. *I'm angry. I'm sad. I'm lonely.*

We practice ordinary attention every moment of every day. We look at a cup, for example, and simply acknowledge, *That's a cup.* Very little judgment is involved at this stage. We don't think *That's a good cup, a bad cup, an attractive cup, a small cup, or a large cup.* We just recognize *cup.* Applying ordinary awareness to thoughts and emotions involves the same simple acknowledgment: *Oh, I'm angry. Oh, I'm jealous. Oh, I'm frustrated. Oh, I could have done better. Oh, I said (or did) something.*

Sometimes, as mentioned earlier, thoughts and emotions are not very clear. In such cases, we can look at the messages we receive from our physical bodies. If we can't sit still or experience physical tension, we can simply look at those sensations. Physical sensations could reflect a host of emotional or mental states—

anger, frustration, jealousy, regret, or a mix of disturbing thoughts and feelings. The important point is to simply look at what's going on and acknowledge whatever you're experiencing just as it is, rather than to resist it or succumb to it.

The second stage involves *meditative awareness*—approaching thoughts and emotions as objects of focus through which we can stabilize awareness. To use an example, a student of mine once confided that he suffered from what he called a "people-pleasing" complex. At work, he was always trying to do more, to work longer hours to complete professional projects, which consequently stole time he wished to spend with his wife and family. The conflict became intense. He would wake up several times during the night, sweating, his heart beating fast. He felt he couldn't please his managers, coworkers, and family at the same time, and the more he tried to please everyone, the less successful he felt. He was judging himself as a failure, creating judgments about others as demanding, and casting those judgments about himself and others in stone. He had succumbed to the first, second, and third of the Buddha Nature Blockers, and locked them in with the fifth. He had defined himself as a failure, incapable of pleasing all of the people all of the time.

This man had some experience with looking at objects, sounds, and physical sensations, so I advised him to apply the same method of meditative awareness during those moments when he woke up at night. "Watch the thoughts, feelings, and physical sensations," I told him. "Initially, 'the people-pleasing' complex might seem like one giant thing. But as you look at the complex it doesn't seem like one big giant thing anymore. You'll start to see that it has a lot of parts. It's made up of thoughts, like 'I should have done A, B, or C. Why didn't I do X, Y, or Z?' It also comprises emotions, such as fear, anger, resentment, and physical sensations, including churning in the stomach, an accelerated heartbeat, and sweating. Images may also occur: people being disappointed in you or yelling at you. As you look with meditative attention, the complex becomes like a bubble—inside of which are many smaller bubbles."

Whatever you're feeling—whether it's panic, anxiety, loneliness, or people-pleasing—the basic approach is to try to watch any of the smaller bubbles with the same sort of attention applied to watching a physical object or focusing on a sound, as described in Part Two. In doing so, you'll probably notice that the thoughts, emotions, and even physical sensations shift and change. For a while, fear may be most persistent, or perhaps the beating of your heart, or the images of people's reactions. After a while—perhaps five minutes or so—one or another of these responses, the bubble within the bubble, pulls your attention. Focus on that with meditative attention. In so doing, gradually your attention will shift from identifying as swallowed up in an emotional bubble to the one watching the bubble.

The third stage of the exercise involves a little bit of analysis: an intuitive "tuning in" to determine the effect of the practice. As I was taught, there are three possible results of applying meditative awareness to an emotional issue.

The first is that the problem dissipates altogether. Some of my students tell me, "You gave me this exercise, but it doesn't work for me."

"What do you mean?" I ask them.

"These thoughts, these emotions, disappear too quickly," they reply. "They become fuzzy or unclear. They don't stay in place long enough to look at them."

"That's great!" I tell them. "That's the point of attention practice."

Many look at me with surprise, until I explain to them that what's happened when they watch thoughts, emotions, or physical sensations, and see them disappear, is that they've arrived at a state of objectless *shamatha*—a point at which one is simply aware of being aware. This objectless state may not last long. Some other thought, emotion, or physical sensation may come up. I urge them to approach the objectless state with the attitude, "Wow, I have another opportunity to develop my awareness of awareness." I encourage them to identify themselves as the "looker."

The second possibility is that the thoughts, feelings, or physical sensations intensify. That's also a good sign—an indication that deeply embedded perspectives are beginning to "loosen up." To use an analogy, suppose you apply a few drops of water to a plate or bowl encrusted with dried food. Initially, the plate or bowl looks messier as the residue spreads. Actually, though, the plate isn't getting messier; the dried food is dissolving.

In terms of meditation practice, when thoughts or feelings intensify, there may be a reluctance to allow them expression. There is nothing wrong with allowing yourself to express an emotion. Perhaps you might want to pound your meditation cushion or say something out loud, like "How could I have done that?" or "Why did this person say that?" One student of mine, who had experienced anger at someone, eventually realized that the anger she felt was actually motivated by hurt that the person in question had acted in a certain way, and she began to cry. Expressing thoughts and emotions can be a great relief. The important point is to maintain your awareness as you express your thoughts or feelings.

The third possibility is that emotions may just remain at the same level, neither diminishing nor intensifying. That's also great! Why? Because we can use an emotion—and the thoughts, images, and physical sensations that accompany it—as strong supports for attention practice. So often, we allow our emotions to use us. Applying attention practice, we use our emotions as a focus for developing awareness, an opportunity to look at the "looker." Just as we need sound to look at sound, form to look at form, we need emotions to look at emotions. In fact, intense emotions can be our best friends in terms of stabilizing the mind, giving the restless bird a branch on which to rest.

Step Two: Try Something Different

In the beginning, it can be difficult to immediately address strong emotions or the biases that have developed over long periods. Emotions can color perception, behavior, even physical sensations. They can seem so solid, so big, that we can't bring ourselves to face them. As one student of mine commented recently, "Working with big emotions—the long-term ones like low self-esteem that kind of define your life—is like trying to climb Mount Everest before we've even learned how to climb a hill."

So, bearing in mind that the goal of *shamatha* practice is to develop stability of awareness, I offer people the advice given to me by my own teachers. Rather than trying to tackle powerful or long-term emotions, focus instead on something smaller and more manageable. For example, a few years ago a woman who suffered from terrible feelings of loneliness asked me to teach her a meditation technique to deal with the issue. When I asked her about her meditation experience, she told me she'd studied for many years under many teachers. I thought, *It's okay to teach her how to use emotion as support for meditation.*

I taught her the attention technique described in Part Two, and she went away with a smile on her face. But a few weeks later, she returned. "I tried my best," she told me, "but I just can't look at this feeling of loneliness. Whenever I try, I feel overwhelmed."

I advised her to go back to the basic exercise of attention practice, turning meditative focus on form and sound. "I don't know how to meditate on form and sound," she answered—a reply I was not expecting. Though, by her own admission, she had attended a lot of teachings, she either hadn't really received much in the way of meditation instruction or had "tuned out" during the teachings of the basic principles.

I gave her basic instruction on paying meditative attention to form and sound. After we practiced these methods for a while, I took a chance, and taught her to focus on smaller emotions—the irritation she felt standing in line at a grocery store or the frustration she might feel confronting a pile of dirty dishes in her kitchen sink. "Try this for a while," I advised. "Then maybe you'll have the strength to look at the larger emotion of loneliness that is troubling you."

A few months later, she wrote to me: "After working this way, I'm now able to start looking at my loneliness and make friends with it."

How do we go about working with smaller or different emotions as a step toward dealing with larger issues?

One method is to generate, by artificial means, another emotion, something simpler or smaller and not so intense. For example, if you're working with loneliness, try working with anger. Imagine a situation in which you're having an argument with a coworker who messed up your files or someone who cuts ahead of you in line at the grocery store. Once you begin to feel that anger, use that to focus your awareness. Focus on the feeling of anger, the words that cross your mind, the physical sensations, or the image of the person cutting ahead of you. Practicing in this way, you can gain experience on how to deal with emotions.

Once you've achieved some proficiency in dealing with artificially generated emotions, you can start to look at past experiences and deliberately recall situations in which you may have felt anger, jealousy, embarrassment, or frustration. Bear in mind that the point of trying something different is to develop a stability of awareness—to discover the looker rather than being overcome by what is looked at.

Working with artificial or smaller emotions builds up the strength to work attentively with larger or long-term emotions, such as loneliness, low self-esteem, or an unhealthy need to please. In a way, this approach is like starting a physical workout regimen. When you go to the gym, you don't start off by lifting heavy weights. You begin by lifting weights that are manageable. Gradually, as your strength improves, you can begin lifting heavier weights. Drawing attention to emotional states works the same way. While there is some benefit in addressing large or long-standing emotional issues directly, sometimes we have to build up our emotional muscles a bit more gradually, remembering that the goal of attention practice is to develop stability of awareness.

Another "Try Something Different" approach involves using the physical symptoms of emotion as objects of focus. For example, a woman attending a public seminar confessed that she had suffered for years from severe depression. She had been taking medication prescribed by her doctor, but she couldn't escape the feeling that her body was filled with burning lead.

"Where do you feel this burning lead?" I asked.

"All over," she replied. "It's overwhelming."

"Okay," I told her. "Instead of looking at the overall pain, focus on one small part of your body. Maybe your foot. Maybe just your toe. Choose a small place to direct your attention. Look at small parts of your body one at a time, instead of trying to work on your whole body at once. Remember that the goal of *shamatha* practice is to develop stability of awareness. Once you've achieved stability by focusing on your foot or your toe, you can begin to extend that awareness to larger areas."

Applying attention to smaller emotions—or simply focusing on form, sound, or physical sensations—develops your capacity to look at long-term, overwhelming emotional states. Once you begin to grow your "attentional muscles" you can begin drawing attention to larger emotional issues. As you do so, you may find yourself directly confronting the underlying Buddha Nature Blockers of self-judgment and judging others as "enemies." You may unravel the belief in being stuck, or the blind spot that inhibits your awareness of your potential. Almost certainly, you will confront the "myth of me," the tendency to identify with your loneliness, low self-esteem, perfectionism, or isolation.

It's important to remember that such confrontations are not battles but opportunities to discover the power of the mind. The same mind that can create such harsh judgments is capable of undoing them through the power of awareness and attention.

Step Three: Step Back

Sometimes an emotion is so persistent or so strong that it just seems impossible to look at. Something holds it in place. Another approach that can be especially helpful when dealing with particularly strong emotions or mental or emotional habits that have developed over a long period is to take a step back and look at what lies behind the emotion—what you might call the support or "booster" of the emotion. For example, there were times when I would try to look directly at the panic I felt as a child, and I just failed. I couldn't sit still, my heart would race, and I'd sweat as my body temperature rose. Finally I asked my teacher, Saljay Rinpoche, for help.

"You don't want to feel panic?" he asked.

"Of course not!" I answered. "I want to get rid of it right now!"

He considered my response for a few moments and then, nodding, replied, "Oh, now I see. What's bothering you is the *fear* of panic. Sometimes, the fear of panic is stronger than the panic itself."

It hadn't occurred to me to step back and look at what might be holding my panic in place. I was too wrapped up in the symptoms to see how very deeply I was afraid of the overwhelming emotion. But as I took Saljay Rinpoche's advice and looked at the underlying fear of panic, I began to find that panic became more manageable.

Over the years, I've found this approach effective in counseling other people. If an emotion or a disturbing state of mind is too painful to look at directly, seek the underlying condition that holds it in place. You may be surprised at what you discover.

You may find fear of the emotion, as I did. You may find some other type of resistance, such as a lack of confidence in even trying to work with emotions. You may find small events, triggers that signal or reinforce a broader emotional response. Fatigue, for example, can often signal a depressive episode. An argument with a coworker, spouse, or family member can often trigger thoughts of worthlessness or isolation, reinforcing a sense of low self-esteem.

When we work with the feelings behind the feelings, we begin to work more directly with the Buddha Nature Blockers—particularly the third, the entrenched belief that we cannot change, the fourth, which denies the possibility of our potential, and the fifth, through which we identify our emotional difficulties.

Step Four: Take a Break

An important part of any practice involves learning when to just stop practicing altogether. Stopping gives you more space, which allows you to accept the ups and downs, the possible turbulence of the experience that may be generated by your practice. If you don't give yourself an opportunity to stop, you may be carried away by the turbulence—and by a sense of guilt because you're not "doing it right" or not understanding the exercise. *How come even though I have these very clear instructions*, you may ask yourself, *they don't seem to work? It must be my fault.*

In general, when you engage in attention practice, you'll encounter two extreme points at which you know when to stop. One extreme is when your practice begins to deteriorate. Maybe you lose your focus or feel disgusted with the exercise. Perhaps the method becomes unclear. Even if you step back, looking at the triggers or boosters of anxiety, loneliness, and so on, or try something different, your practice doesn't work. You may think, *I'm so tired of practicing altogether. I can't see the benefit of going on.*

I met a young woman recently who had such an experience. She tried meditating on her perpetual anxiety. For a while, her practice seemed successful and she was happy about it. Then, it didn't seem to work. Her anxiety intensified, and her ability to focus diminished. One day, she attended a guided group meditation I was leading. At the beginning of the session she seemed fine; but at the end she was crying and shifting around on her meditation cushion. After the group meditation concluded, she made an appointment with me for a private interview.

"Your methods work for me," she began, "but over the past few days, I'm unclear, confused, tired, bored, and at the end of the group meditation, I just felt myself collapsing. I'm done with this practice. I just can't seem to get it. I'm thinking of joining a support group, where they allow you to just cry your heart out."

After she finished, I explained to her that sometimes it's necessary to stop practicing for a while—to just do something else. Take a walk. Read a book. Watch TV or listen to music. She went to her room that night, slept, and in the morning felt a little bit better. She wanted to try the exercise again—knowing that she could stop whenever she needed to. She didn't have to keep going as if she were running a race or involved in some sort competition.

The idea of stopping meditation when the focus becomes too intense or your mind becomes dull or confused is actually an important and often overlooked part of practice. An analogy is often drawn from "dry channel" or "empty reservoir" irrigation practices implemented by Tibetan farmers who would plant their fields around a natural reservoir, such as a small pond or lake, around which they'd dig channels that would run through the crops. Sometimes, even if the channels were well dug, there wasn't much water flowing through them, because the reservoir itself was empty.

Similarly, when you practice, even though you have clear instructions and you understand the importance of effort and intention, you can experience fatigue, irritation, dullness, or hopelessness because your mental, emotional, and physical "reservoir" is empty. The likely cause is that you've applied too much effort, too eagerly, and haven't built up a sufficiently abundant reservoir of inner strength. The instructions I received from my father and other teachers urging short practice periods can't be emphasized enough. In dealing with intense or long-term emotional states, we need to fill our reservoirs. Even the Buddha didn't become the Buddha overnight!

The second extreme at which it's important to take a break occurs when your experience of the practice feels absolutely fantastic. There may come a point at which you feel extraordinarily light and comfortable in your body or an intense state of happiness or joy. You may experience a boundless sense of clarity—a mental experience like a brilliant sun shining in a cloudless blue sky. Everything appears so fresh and precise. Or perhaps thoughts, feelings, and sensations cease and your mind becomes completely still. At this point, you stop.

Sometimes people say, "It's not fair! I'm having such a wonderful experience. Why should I stop?"

I sympathize with their frustration, since I, too, have enjoyed such blissful experiences. I felt such greed, such desire to hold on to them. But my teachers explained to me that if I held on, I would eventually grow disappointed. Because the nature of experience is impermanent, sooner or later the bliss, the clarity, the stillness, and so on, would vanish, and then I would feel really horrible. I'd end up feeling like I did something wrong or that the practices don't work. While the real goal is to develop a stability of awareness that allows one to look with equanimity at any experience, there is also the danger of becoming attached to blissful, clear, or still experiences as the result of attention practice.

They further explained that taking a break at a high point cultivates an eagerness to continue practicing, encouraging us to stabilize awareness, and "build up our reservoirs."

Strange as it may seem, stopping is as much an important aspect of practice as starting.

BREAKING IT DOWN

The primordial purity of the ground completely transcends words, concepts, and formulations.

—Jamgön Kongtrul, *Myriad Worlds*,
translated and edited by the International Committee
of Kunkhyab Chöling

A woman who'd attended a series of teachings during one of my recent visits to North America confessed in a private talk that, while she had accomplished many things in her life, she felt a deep longing for a lasting relationship. This longing was so intense that she couldn't even look at it in meditation.

When asked what kind of thoughts she had when she experienced this longing for a relationship, she sat quietly for a few moments, and then replied, "I guess the thought that I'm unlovable." After another pause she added, in a smaller voice, "And maybe the idea that other people will think I'm a failure because I've never had a long-term relationship."

Continuing this line of questioning uncovered a variety of different thoughts and feelings—including memories of childhood (her mother telling her she was ugly) and adolescence (not being invited to dances and parties). There was, in fact, an entire storyline beneath her longing for a relationship. And when this storyline was broken down into its various parts, the heaviness of her longing began to lift. It didn't disappear right away, of course, but in those moments, it became lighter to bear. It wasn't the overwhelmingly huge, solid, muddy rock she'd originally been carrying around. It was really more of a bunch of stones clumped together in a way that looked like a big rock.

Without exertion, she began, spontaneously, to apply method and wisdom to her sadness. This is a critical point. As she considered each aspect of her predicament, she was *meditating,* acknowledging on a direct level thoughts and feelings that had plagued her for much of her life. As she acknowledged them, some of the judgment she'd held about these thoughts and feelings began to lift, and she was able to break them down into smaller and smaller pieces. Over the course of the discussion, she experienced, at least momentarily, a shift in perspective. She wasn't someone trapped within the mirror of her loneliness and longing. She was the mirror.

Toward the end of the conversation, she gasped.

"I just had a thought," she said. "Maybe my mother felt the same way. Maybe she felt ugly and unlovable. I don't remember ever seeing her happy or smiling. I don't remember seeing my parents laugh together, or embrace, or kiss. And those other kids I grew up with, the popular ones, the ones who got invited to dances and parties . . ."

Her voice trailed off for a moment.

"Were their lives all that great back then?" she asked. She chewed her lip, considering. "Are they happy now? Do they feel alone?"

It was extraordinary to watch this process unfold. Admitting her secret pain allowed her awareness to expand in a manner that enabled her to simply look at it with less judgment than she had while keeping it hidden. In turn, that awareness helped her to break the pain into smaller pieces, so it didn't seem so fixed; and releasing that fixation provided the opportunity for her innate compassion, capability, and confidence to begin to bloom. And at least in those few moments, her mythology of "me"—of being singularly focused on her own perspective—melted. She didn't feel lonely, unloved, and unlovable; and she began to experience a connection to others that transcended desire, jealousy, and fear. She befriended her pain, and in so doing arrived at insight and empathy. She'd glimpsed her potential, embraced the change in her perspective, and for a moment, at least, felt free. The smile on her face after this spontaneous breakthrough was a delight to behold.

This is the point of insight practice: the recognition that all phenomena are interdependent, impermanent, and made up of many different parts. As discussed in Part One, upon examination, we can't point to anything as solid, singular, or unchangeable. The more deeply we examine our thoughts, feelings, and emotions, the greater the opportunity we have to recognize their empty nature. Even intense or long-term emotional states are like bubbles. They seem to have a form but they're empty inside. In the end, they pop and you can see boundless space, free from conflicts and collisions. It's a joyful awakening, which, though you can't put it into words, is totally clear, an experience of timeless awareness.

How do we approach this awakening? By taking certain steps, just as we did in approaching attention practice.

Step One: The Main Exercise

Like the main exercise of attention practice, insight meditation can be broken down into three stages. The first involves looking at a thought or emotion with ordinary awareness—simply identifying thoughts or feelings without any specific purpose or intention.

Stage two involves a somewhat different approach. The main idea is to recognize the nature of the emotion, which is that awareness is inseparable from emptiness. How do we do this?

Begin by considering the impermanent aspect of emotion. When we identify an emotion—whether it's self-hatred, loneliness, a feeling of awkwardness in social situations, or a judgment against another person—we tend to think of it as a big, solid problem. A sense of permanence surrounds and infuses the feeling. *I will always feel this way. I'm a loser. That person really is bad.* Buddha Nature Blocker number three plays a prominent role here, enforcing a sense of endurability. But when we carefully examine such feelings, we find they're not stable or enduring at all. In a minute or less the thoughts associated with them change, the intensity wavers. Physical sensations—body temperature, heartbeat, heaviness in the limbs, fatigue, or agitation—are apt to shift. We may be surprised at the many different changes in the mind and body. Building on the process of attention practice, the essential point here is to observe and allow ourselves to become aware of the changes.

In the beginning we may be able to observe the shifts in thoughts, feelings, and so on, for only a minute or two. That's okay. As my own teachers advised me, it's important to resist the impulse to strive for a result. The main point of recognizing impermanence is to simply notice that thoughts, feelings, and physical changes are not static.

After looking briefly at the impermanent nature of emotions, consider their singularity aspect. As mentioned earlier, we tend to experience emotion as a big, solid, inherently existing thing. But if we look closely at the emotion—for example, anger—we can see that it is a combination of words or thoughts (*I'm angry. I hate that person. That was a horrible thing to say*), physical sensations (pain, tightness in the chest or stomach), and the image of the cause or object of anger. If we separate all these out, where is the anger? Is it possible to experience anger without words, thoughts, physical sensations, or images of the cause or object?

Or, to take a different approach, suppose we look at the object of anger—for example, someone who says something we don't like. We can ask, *What's making me angry? The person who said the words? The words themselves?* We may think, *I'm angry at a specific person because of what he or she said.* But if we take a moment to break down our response, we allow ourselves the opportunity to reconsider, to take a second look. *The bad words came from this person's mouth, so should I be angry at his or her mouth? That person's mouth is controlled by his or her muscles and brain. Should I be angry at the muscles and the brain? And are the muscles of the brain motivated by that person's emotions or his or her intentions? Should I be angry at those?* Examining singularity in this way, we can't find any object to be angry at. The object of anger does not have any nature of its own. Instead, we find that emotions and their objects arise interdependently.

I saw this for myself as a child, when a man came to visit my father. He'd had an argument with someone and they'd ended up beating each other with sticks. The man was very upset and asked my father for advice.

My father said, "It was the stick that hit you; why are you angry at the other man?"

"Because he controlled the stick," the fellow replied.

"But he was controlled by his emotions," my father told him. "So really you should be angry at his emotions. And who knows what might have contributed to his emotional outburst? Maybe he was beaten by his father. Maybe something happened that day to make him angry. So who can you be angry at? Maybe the man's father beat this man you argued with out of anger. But who knows what made him so angry that he beat his son?"

The man thought for a while, and I saw him begin to relax a bit, and even begin to smile.

"I never thought about it that way," he said.

"Most of us don't," my father replied. "We have to look beyond surface appearances, and that takes practice." He smiled. "And practice takes time. Just because we talked today, your ideas, your emotions, aren't going to change overnight. Be patient. Be kind to yourself. You can't gain wisdom overnight."

My father's words stuck with me, and I bear them in mind when I teach and counsel others. The main exercise of insight practice consists of examining the impermanence and interdependence of our own emotional responses and of the objects of our emotions—people, places, and situations. Even as we break down loneliness, lovelessness, social discomfort, judgment of others, and so on, into separate parts, we begin to see that even the parts cannot be said to inherently exist.

That is the goal of insight practice: to break down the illusion of permanence, singularity, and independence. If we look at emotion this deeply, eventually we'll arrive at the conclusion that we can't find any permanent, singular, or independent factor. The emotion or its object may dissipate with practice. More importantly, as we approach our thoughts and feelings with insight, we can discover the nature of emotion, an unlimited clarity and freedom, previously unrecognized. To be able to choose our responses, to loosen the boundary between experience and experiencer—what a discovery!

A traditional Tibetan Buddhist analogy likens this experience to a traveler wearing a wide-brimmed hat while walking up a steep hill that's lined with trees. Upon reaching the top of the hill, he removes his hat and rests on the ground. He enjoys the sensation of the wind blowing across his head, revels in the capacity to see for miles and to stare at the wide, open sky. He cherishes the relief of having reached the top of the hill. The hat represents the aggregate of the concepts to which we cling when we think of emotions as solid, permanent, independently existing. The trek up the hill represents the process of looking at the nature of emotions. The removal of the hat represents not only the relief of letting go of the concepts, but also the unbounded awareness that results.

A note of caution is appropriate here, though. The sense of freedom and awareness you achieve through insight practice may last only a few seconds, a gap in the more-or-less continuous flow of conceptual awareness. Don't worry. Though the gap may be short initially, it actually represents a glimpse of the natural state of mind—a union of emptiness and clarity. With practice, the gap will grow longer and longer.

As with attention practice, the third stage of the insight meditation involves a little bit of analysis. When you look at the results of your practice you may experience, as with attention practice, three possible results.

First, when you look at an emotion, it may dissolve into boundless awareness for a short period, maybe just a few seconds. Then the emotion will return, possibly more intensely. You may think, *I'm still here, I'm feeling the emotion, what's the point in trying to see this emotion as empty?* That's normal. You can always return to the practice. There's no time limit, no instruction that forbids you from trying five, six, seven, or even a hundred times a day. In fact, my teachers advised me to keep trying, even if only for short periods of a minute or so. Gradually, through repetition, you'll discover that a particular emotion becomes less and less solid, and transforms into boundless awareness. One day, when the emotion arises, it will remind you of the freedom and spaciousness of what you've come to experience during practice. Rather than dragging you down, the experience of loneliness, lovelessness, anger, and so on, will lift you up.

The second possibility is that when you apply insight practice, the emotion becomes more intense. You may feel like you can't watch this emotion because it's so strong or so real. *I failed. I feel this emotion too vividly.* That's okay, too. It's actually a sign of enhanced clarity. Don't try to get rid of the emotion. See all the different parts—how they change, how they are impermanent. It may not exactly become insight meditation, but it will be a more profound experience of attention.

The third possibility is that when you look at the emotion it just stays the same—neither intensifying nor dissipating. You may see emotion and the emptiness at the same time. When you feel desire, for example, or jealousy, and look at that desire or jealousy, you may discover a lingering "flavor"—an echo, so to speak, like the feeling you experience in a dream. A traditional Buddhist metaphor likens such experience to seeing a reflection in a puddle or a mirror. You can see your reflection but you don't mistake it for yourself. According to my teachers, this is the best result, a sign of liberation of emotion. Though you may still sense it, you have a clear understanding of its empty nature.

Step Two: Try Something Different

Of course, some emotional or mental states are very strong or persistent, as demonstrated by the case of the woman who had spent so much of her life longing for a relationship, or, in today's economic climate, someone's pervasive sense of insecurity. Sometimes rage against a parent or other family member—or perhaps a coworker—can last for years. I've found this especially true among people who have been divorced or are currently involved in divorce proceedings. Depression, anxiety, regret over past actions tend to extend over long periods as well. Any of these states can be difficult to tackle head-on.

Instead of trying to deal with these "heavy hitters" right away, try working with something that's a bit easier to break down. You might try to create an artificial sense of physical pain, for example, by pinching the fleshy area between the thumb and forefinger. Working with that simple level of discomfort is very simple and direct. (A side benefit, according to experts in acupressure, is that applying such pressure relieves headaches.) Or you might try working with sensations of extreme heat or cold, drawing upon memories of sensations to work with the discomfort of sweating, shivering, and the wish to relieve such conditions. Another possibility is to look at your desire for something, like a technical gadget.

Another approach may involve breaking down a large emotion into smaller pieces. A student who had suffered recurring bouts of depression described an innovative method of practicing insight. The trigger that launched most of her depressive episodes was a repetition of a message she'd heard from her mother early on in her childhood: "You're a mess." When this statement repeated itself in her mind, she began to cut it into little pieces. "You're a m—" "You're a." "You're." "You." "Y—" After applying this method, she found the freedom to question the meaning of her thoughts and feelings. *What is "a mess"? What is "You are"? What is "You"?*

What or who was my mother to make such a pronouncement? Who was "she" to accept the definition of "herself" as a mess?

You might find it helpful to try a more analytical approach to breaking down large emotions into smaller pieces. For example, when you're jealous, ask yourself, *Who is jealous? Is it my foot? My hand? Where does jealousy arise? Does it endure? Is the jealousy interrupted by other thoughts or feelings? Who is the person I'm jealous of? Am I jealous of his or her hand or foot? His or her mouth? The words coming out of his or her mouth? Can I actually identify a permanent, singular, independent entity of whom I'm jealous?*

A different approach involves looking at childhood memories, which are often more easily broken down than the complex thoughts and feelings that burden us in adulthood. You might, as one student I spoke with recently did, recall an experience of falling out of a tree and skinning your knee. He experienced not only physical pain but a sense of embarrassment that so many of his fellow playmates had seen him fall. *What did the physical pain feel like?* he asked himself. *What did the embarrassment feel like? Did my heart race? Did I feel blood rush to my face? Did I want to run and hide?*

The point of trying something different in terms of insight meditation is *practice*. Start small and use a focus that is somewhat easy. In so doing you build your strength—or, to return to the old Tibetan metaphor, fill your reservoir—so that you can work with larger or more persistent issues.

Step Three: Step Back

Many people resist insight practice. Some find it difficult to break down emotions into smaller pieces. Others find the practice too dry or analytical. Some are simply too afraid to look at the underlying source of their emotions. For example, a student of mine recently spoke about a conflict he was having with his mother. Every time his mother needed to fill up the gas tank of her car, she would call him to come help her. On the surface the conflict seemed to revolve around his mother's helplessness, but when he finally confronted her, together they discovered that the underlying issues were a combination of jealousy and grief. His mother was jealous over the time he was spending with his roommate, and she was suffering from a sense of loss in the aftermath of her son moving out of her home to live on his own.

As this example demonstrates, one of the strongest factors in resisting insight practice is the fear of change, the fear of losing your identity—a reflection of the influence of Buddha Nature Blocker number five, the tendency to identify, for example, as someone helpless, lonely, anxious, or afraid. The mother in the example just mentioned was afraid of losing her relationship with her son. Other people have told me, "I need my anger to get things done." Another student spoke to me recently about her relationship with a songwriter, who frequently engaged in arguments, repeatedly broke off his relationship with her, and then made efforts to repair the relationship. Their relationship was a constant source of pain and drama, love, and loss. Finally, she asked her partner, "Can't we just have a middling relationship, without all these ups and downs? Of course, we'll have disagreements, but do they have to be so dramatic? Does every upset have to be life-or-death?" He looked at her for a moment as if she were an alien from another planet. "I need emotional drama in order to be creative," he replied. "The ups and downs of a relationship—I need them in order to write my lyrics."

Fortunately for her, she didn't need the drama to fulfill her own professional needs or obligations, and after that discussion she ended the relationship.

I found her story especially illuminating, however, because many people resist insight practice out of a misunderstanding of emptiness. More than one person has asked me, "If I'm empty, if everyone I work with is empty, if all my feelings are empty, how can I function in social life?" They're afraid that they'll have to abandon their identities or that their relationships and experiences will become meaningless.

Questions like these remind me of a couple of incidents from my early childhood. Most of my early years were spent in Nubri, an area in the Himalayan region of Nepal where winter storms can be very harsh. During one particularly severe storm when the north wind blew so strongly against the walls of our house, I was so terrified the house would blow down. I ran to one of the pillars in the main room and pressed with all my strength against the wind. (The house didn't collapse, of course, but I doubt if my puny efforts played any part.)

I then compare this experience to an incident that occurred a couple of years later, when I took my first bus ride. One winter, I traveled with my mother from Nubri, which at that time was an isolated village with no modern conveniences—no running water, no electricity, and no paved roads—to Katmandu, where the weather was warmer and we could spend the winter in relative warmth and comfort. We walked for ten days through a pristine, undeveloped environment, sleeping at night in caves or in the fields and cooking our meals with supplies that we carried on our backs. Then we reached a place called Gorka. There, for the first time, I encountered trucks and buses.

My first impression was that they were giant animals. The headlights looked like eyes. They growled as they moved. Their horns roared like angry tigers. As we approached one bus, my mother said, "We have to go in there."

No way, I thought. But my mother was adamant, and she pulled me onto the bus. The first day of the ride I was terrified. I was sitting inside the belly of a beast! The roads on which we traveled were terrible—full of bumps and potholes—and every time we hit one, I was sure the beast would flip over. After a few hours, I got dizzy and vomited. At last we came to a stop, and my mother and I checked into a hotel. That night, I developed a fever and became dizzy again. I remember looking up at the ceiling fan, which wasn't turned on, and thinking I saw the blades turning. Gradually, the whole room began to spin.

The next day I felt a bit better, and my mother told me in no uncertain terms, "We have to go." As we climbed aboard the bus, my mother settled us in the front seat. I began to tell myself—almost like a *mantra*—that this is just a horse, it's not a wild beast. Slowly, my experience of riding the bus began to change. I knew horses. I'd ridden them before. I opened the window and felt the breeze blowing across my face. I looked out and began to take in the view of green trees and grass as we traveled through the south of Nepal. It looked and felt like summer.

Through looking at my fear and shifting my perception, I made peace with riding on the bus. More importantly, the experience was one of my first exercises in insight practice, which is essentially a process of letting go of preconceived notions, embracing change, and breaking through the "blind spot" to discover inner resources that I never dreamed possible.

Step Four: Take a Break

Even if you try all of the steps described here, you can find that your practice becomes unclear. You may grow tired, frustrated, or bored. You may lose enthusiasm even for taking a minute or two out of your day to practice.

To use an analogy, people who take up jogging may be able to run for only five or ten minutes at first. Even during such short workouts, they may need to pause for a while; and if they want to continue longer, they can't, because their bodies are simply not used to the exertion. They have to stop no matter how much they may wish to continue. They may try the next day and the next, extending their workout a little longer. Eventually they are able to go on for many miles and might even be able to run a marathon! Similarly, it's important to take a break when engaging in insight practice—especially if you become bored or uninterested, if the practice seems too dry or analytical, or if the emotions you're exploring intensify.

As with attention practice, it's also imperative to stop if the feelings dissipate or you attain a really deep experience of emptiness, through which dualistic perception dissolves. When they hear this, many people wonder, "Why should I stop when the practice seems to be working so well?"

I asked the same question of my own teachers, and I offer the same reply. It's so easy to become attached to the sensation of freedom that we may be tempted to manufacture it. Letting go of feelings of release or relief is the ultimate exercise of insight. We're letting go of letting go.

EXTENDING EMPATHY

*Immense compassion springs forth spontaneously toward all
sentient beings who suffer as prisoners of their illusions.*

—Kalu Rinpoche, *Luminous Mind: The Way
of the Buddha*, translated by Maria Montenegro

Several months ago, a student of mine broke her pelvis after falling
off a horse. While she was recovering, her boyfriend ended their
relationship. Through phone calls and e-mails, he criticized her for
"playing the victim" and trying to gain sympathy. He told her that
her accident was a result of "bad karma" because she had disturbing relationships with her family. Throughout the process, she refused to talk about his response, making her ex-boyfriend into a
"bad guy" in the eyes of friends and family, and reinforcing that
judgment in her own mind.

In an odd coincidence, three months after ending the relationship, her ex-boyfriend fell from a tree and broke several bones in
his back.

My student could have responded negatively when he called to
ask her to return some devices he'd sent her to relieve her physical
pain. Instead, she made a care package, including the requested
devices along with homeopathic remedies that had helped her endure her pain. Having recognized the emotional pain of being attacked while suffering severe physical pain, she chose to take what
some people call the "high road." Instead of asking him if he was
playing the victim or if his accident was the result of bad karma,
she recognized the emotional pain she'd felt and chose to extend
herself by sending a care package.

Rather than fighting with her ex-boyfriend, she responded empathetically, experiencing a peace of mind while extending to her boyfriend not only the opportunity of peace but also the chance to appreciate the possibility of recognizing what he'd done in judging her. Had she responded angrily, throwing his accusations back at him, it's likely he would have closed his mind and become bitter or more harshly judgmental. By choosing to extend herself by preparing a care package instead of retaliating, she not only experienced an opening of her heart, she also offered her ex-boyfriend the opportunity to open his—that is, to recognize that attacking someone in pain is probably not the best approach to establishing and promoting healthy relationships.

Step One: The Main Exercise

As with the main exercise of attention and insight practice, empathy meditation can be broken down into several stages. While attention and insight practice can be condensed into three stages, empathy has a different flavor. It's a transformational process. So rather than three stages, extending empathy includes a fourth stage, as we shall see.

The first stage is similar to that of attention and insight practice—that is, to simply draw awareness to whatever you're feeling. The second stage involves recognizing that other people suffer from overwhelming emotions or emotional conflicts, a realization, in effect, that "I'm not the only one who suffers." As you understand other people's suffering in this way, then you begin to feel that you and others are the same. Just as you want to be free from suffering, so do others; just as you want to achieve happiness, so do others. Perhaps you may recall the analogy described in Part Two, in which you imagine your cheeks with two very sharp needles stuck in them, one in the left cheek and one in the right. The pain in the right cheek represents the unhappiness and suffering you experience yourself. The pain in the left cheek represents the pain and unhappiness experienced by others. The pain in both cheeks is equal.

The third stage of the main practice involves the practice of *tonglen,* which was described in detail in Part Two. To briefly summarize this technique, you begin by drawing attention to your own suffering, recognize that others suffer, and then use your imagination to draw into yourself all the suffering and painful emotions and situations experienced by countless sentient beings. Then you imagine sending out all your good qualities, all your experiences of momentary happiness, to others. Some texts advise imagining the suffering as a thick, black cloud, and the happiness and positive qualities as a bright ray of light. As a reminder, you can coordinate the taking and sending process with your breath, inhaling as you take in other sentient beings' suffering, and exhaling as you imagine sending out your positive qualities. Many of my students have reported that coordinating the visualization process with the breath produces a calming effect of its own.

The practice of *tonglen* has many benefits. The first, of course, is the recognition that you're not alone, which helps to relieve the personal suffering based on self-judgment. Second, recognizing the suffering of others helps to dissolve judgments against them, some of which may be long-standing. As you acknowledge your own pain and some of the words, images, and behaviors that arise as a result, you begin to recognize that some of the actions of others, which may seem hurtful or uncaring, arise from a similar well of unhappiness. Extending your positive qualities, meanwhile, helps to undercut the influence of Buddha Nature Blocker number four—the blind spot—gradually bringing to conscious awareness the fact that you do have positive qualities, and perhaps broader capabilities than you might previously have imagined.

Most importantly, however, by applying this particular approach to empathy, you'll gradually begin to develop a sense that your personal suffering is meaningful or has a purpose. As you begin to see your emotion as a representation of all sentient beings' emotions, you are deepening your commitment to connect and to help other sentient beings become free from disturbing or destructive emotions.

Stage four of the main practice is a little different from the analytical process associated with attention and insight practice. Here, we're looking at the transformational power of empathy. Rather than running from emotion, attempting to suppress it, or letting it overtake you, you can let it arise. As the emotion occurs, it becomes part of loving-kindness and compassion, and then it becomes productive. With practice, you'll discover a natural shift in perspective regarding disturbing emotions. They're not bad things, not harmful; these unpleasant emotions are actually beneficial to your pursuit of becoming more acutely aware of others' suffering. And by using them as a focus of *tonglen* practice you end up helping others.

Step Two: Try Something Different

As mentioned earlier in the discussion of attention and insight practice, it may not be easy to work directly with intense emotions or long-term patterns. If you find a similar problem when working with empathy, try working with a smaller emotion or perhaps only one aspect of an intense or long-term emotional pattern. Intense emotions or entrenched emotional patterns lie deep within us—

like oceans that seem to have no bottom or end. Before trying to swim across an ocean, it may be more effective to begin to build up your strength by practicing in a pool or a pond.

For example, if you suffer from low self-esteem, loneliness, anxiety, or depression, don't try to tackle all the conditions at once. Focus on one aspect—perhaps your response to something said that triggered a sense of self-judgment or a feeling of hopelessness or fatigue that presages an onset of a depressive episode.

You might begin by using a smaller emotion, like the frustration or irritation you feel toward someone who cuts ahead of you at the grocery store checkout or the line at the bank. Another option may be to work with ordinary loving-kindness/compassion. A man who suffered from persistent anxiety chose this route. When he suffered an anxiety attack, he focused on his grandmother, who was a very anxious person. Through identifying with her, his own anxiety abated, and gradually he was able to extend empathy toward a wider range of people. Recalling a past emotion—such as fear or anger—or even the pain and embarrassment of falling out of a tree, as mentioned earlier—can also help you build up the strength to deal with larger emotions. Once you build up your strength in these small ways, you can begin to work with larger issues of self-judgment and judging others.

Step Three: Step Back

Normally, when we consider practicing empathy, we think we have to put aside negative emotions, ego, etc. But by using the practice of *tonglen,* we discover that negative emotions have a whole different side or aspect. For example, one woman told me during a private interview that she had a bad temper and asked me for a method to control it. I began by teaching her *shamatha*—developing awareness of her temper. She interrupted me, saying, "I tried that already; it doesn't work for me. I need something different." So I taught her *tonglen* meditation, and at first she was surprised. "What a nice idea!" she exclaimed. But after thinking about it for a few moments, she said, "I don't think that's going to work because compassion is the opposite of my temperament. I really have a hard time even conceiving of compassion." I advised her to just try it. "Come back tomorrow, and let me know what happened."

The next morning, she returned, beaming. "I surprised myself. Normally, when I try to meditate on compassion, I'm fighting with my temper. I'm trying to resist and suppress it. But with this technique, I just allowed my bad temper to be there. I didn't change it, I changed the way I viewed it."

Her response inspired me to look at why so many people resist extending empathy. The first problem results from a misunderstanding of the intention behind the method—using the technique to get rid of emotion. You may think, *I have a problem with judging or blaming others. Now I'm going to practice so I can break free from this pattern, right now, right here.* But that doesn't happen. It doesn't go away. You think, *Oh, no, I'm stuck!* or *I hate this practice. It doesn't work.*

Such reactions are classic examples of the involvement of hope and fear—hope that the emotion will just go away and fear that no amount of effort will change your emotional state. As my teacher, Saljay Rinpoche, advised me early on when I was dealing with panic, you need to step back and look at hope and fear as focuses of empathy practice. We all hope for relief from suffering and fear that nothing we do can relieve it.

The second type of resistance comes from looking at the emotion itself. Loneliness, low self-esteem, the judgments we hold against others, and so on, may just seem too large or too deeply entrenched to confront directly. If that's the case, take a step back and try working with smaller emotions. Work with the triggers or boosters or perhaps childhood memories. Look at hope and fear.

Step Four: Take a Break

As with the previous practices of attention and insight, it's possible that you can become bored or tired. *Oh, no*, you might think, *I have to try again*. Perhaps the point of the practice becomes unclear and your enthusiasm diminishes. These are clear signals to stop. There's no need to feel guilty. Remember, you're building your mental and emotional muscles, and that takes time.

As I've advised when practicing attention and insight, it's also important to stop when your practice seems to proceed well. When you feel that loving-kindness and compassion have developed to fantastic levels—when you feel, *From today on, I can serve all sentient beings forever; I'm really transformed; I can give all my goodness away*—it's time to stop.

Why?

Perhaps an example drawn from Buddhist history may provide an explanation. During the nineteenth century, a great Tibetan Buddhist master, Patrul Rinpoche—after spending much of his early life in deep meditation and receiving instructions from some of the most important teachers and scholars of his day—became a teacher.

After receiving basic teachings on loving-kindness and compassion, one of his students excitedly announced, "Now I understand loving-kindness and compassion! From today on, I feel a complete release from fear and anger. Even if someone beats me I'm not going to be upset!

Patrul Rinpoche quietly advised him, "It's too early to jump to such a conclusion. Take it easy. Just practice."

But the student didn't agree and began announcing his transformation to anyone who would listen.

One morning, he sat meditating by a *stupa*—a spiritual monument representing the enlightened mind of the Buddha. He was facing east, the direction of the rising sun, and wearing his outer robe over his head while he meditated with his eyes half-closed. At the same time, Patrul Rinpoche was circling the *stupa,* which is a devotional act. As was his custom, he abstained from wearing rich ceremonial clothes and was simply wearing ripped robes full of holes and made of cheap material. After his first circuit of the *stupa* he stopped in front of his student and asked him, "Sir, what are you doing here?"

Not recognizing his teacher in such poor garments, the student tersely replied, "I'm meditating on loving-kindness and compassion."

"Oh, how nice," Patrul Rinpoche said.

After making another circuit around the *stupa,* Patrul Rinpoche again confronted his student, asking him what he was doing.

The student—still not recognizing his teacher—answered, a bit more curtly, "I'm *meditating* on loving-kindness and compassion."

"That's very nice," Patrul Rinpoche replied.

After one more circuit, he paused before his student and asked the same question. This time, his student shouted angrily, "I told you I'm meditating on loving-kindness and compassion! What's wrong with you? Don't you have ears!" At that moment, as the student shook with anger, his robe slipped from his head, he opened his eyes fully, and he recognized his teacher.

Patrul Rinpoche stood before him smiling. "That was your compassion?" he asked mildly.

In that moment, the student lost all his pride.

The moral of the story is that even if we achieve a little bit of intellectual understanding of empathy and achieve some small result though practice, we still need time to increase the capacity for loving-kindness and compassion. And that requires knowing when to take a break and practicing for very short periods—maybe a minute or so, several times a day—until our "emotional muscles of compassion" develop.

IN CONCLUSION

In meditation, as in all arts, there has to be a delicate balance. . . .

—Sogyal Rinpoche, *The Tibetan Book of Living and Dying*
edited by Patrick Gaffney and Andrew Harvey

A few years ago, during a long stay in the New York City area, I met a man who wanted to learn about meditation. His best friend had died a while earlier and, as a result, he was suffering from grief, depression, and constant fear about his own death. Over a few weeks during a series of private interviews, I taught him how to use form and other sensory supports for meditation and gave him special homework to improve those sensory aspects of meditation. Later, during a public teaching, he learned how to use thoughts and emotions as supports for meditation. Shortly after that public teaching, he asked for another interview.

"I can't watch thoughts and emotions," he confessed. "It's too scary, like watching a tsunami coming at me."

I knew a little bit about his background, and I thought his choice of image in describing emotions rather interesting.

"Remind me," I asked him, "what's your main occupation in life?"

"I'm a professional surfer," he murmured.

"Yes, now I remember," I replied. "So, what do you think about big waves?"

"Oh, I like big waves!" he exclaimed.

I nodded. "So, tell me how you learned to surf. Did you like waves before then?"

The man explained that he was encouraged by some friends who were avid surfers. It took quite a while to persuade him because even small waves seemed threatening, like "tsunamis"—the same word he'd used to describe emotions.

"But with the help of my friends, I pushed myself past the fear and now I love waves. I can play in them. I can use waves as fun. Even the big ones, they seem like a challenge, a way to push myself farther and improve my skill. In fact, riding the waves is pretty much how I make my living nowadays, entering competitions and earning prizes. I guess you could say," he added excitedly, "that waves are my life!"

I waited a moment until he'd finished his story, enjoying the smile that had widened as he talked about his profession. Then I told him, "Your thoughts and emotions are like waves. Riding waves is like watching thoughts and emotions. So if you know how to use waves, as you said, you also have a basic understanding of how to ride your thoughts and emotions."

I then gave him a bit of homework. He was to start small and work slowly with his thoughts and emotions, just as he'd worked with waves when he first began to surf. "The practices are like your friends," I said. "Their aim is to encourage you, to help you face the waves of thoughts and emotions as something to play with. You can't stop waves from rising, can you? But you can learn to ride them."

I didn't see the man for another year, but when I met him again, he had a big smile on his face.

"Remember when I told you that waves were my life?" he asked.

"Yes, certainly," I replied.

"Well, now thoughts and emotions are my life! You were right; it's just like surfing."

"What method did you use?" I asked.

"All of them," he said. "Sometimes I switch them, just like I switch my approach to surfing. You know, sometimes long boarding or short boarding, floating, and curving, going off the lip."

Since I'm not a professional surfer myself, I didn't understand any of the terms he mentioned. But I was able to grasp a key point of his explanation: the importance of switching methods.

As my own teachers pointed out to me early on, it's imperative to shift your focus—both in terms of method and the object or support—from time to time in order to keep your practice fresh. If you settle on one object or method for too long, you can grow bored, unclear, exhausted. A number of people I've met have lost their enthusiasm for practice because they've stuck so long with one method that seemed to work for them.

One man I encountered some time ago had been working exclusively for many years focusing on his breath as a calming exercise and a means of coming to grips with impermanence. "The first year was great," he told me. "But many years later, I don't feel the same effect. I don't feel like I'm moving forward or getting any deeper or growing. When I'm busy and a lot of thoughts come up, breathing meditation used to work so well to calm me down, but now it doesn't help at all."

As we talked, I learned that he'd been taught only that one technique. So I advised him that he might find some relief by trying other methods. Over a few days, I taught him the basic steps of attention, insight, and loving-kindness/compassion practices. I further recommended that he periodically switch his approach. Every time we meet, he thanks me for opening his eyes to the fact that there are a number of possible ways to work with his mind.

"Don't thank me," I tell him. "Thank those who came before. My teachers, their teachers, and the Buddhist masters of bygone ages understood that emotions arise and are held in place by Buddha Nature Blockers, which are essentially habits of perception that spring to life at birth and become stronger and more deeply entrenched as we grow. These five perspectives lock us into a certain type of identity, a way of relating to ourselves and others that is at best disturbing and at worst destructive. When we work with different methods, we begin to understand their influence. And in understanding their influence, we begin to recognize the power and potential of our own mind. That is the true basis of Buddhist practice: understanding the capacity of the mind to create its own perception of the reality in which we function."

12

JOYFUL WISDOM

You will succeed if you persevere; and you will find a joy in overcoming obstacles.

—HELEN KELLER

WITHIN OUR PERCEIVED weaknesses and imperfections lies the key to realizing our true strength. By facing our disturbing emotions and the problems that occur in our lives, we discover an experience of well-being that extends outward as well as inward. Had I not faced the panic and anxiety I felt through most of my youth, I would not be in the position in which I find myself today. I would never have found the courage or the strength to get on a plane, travel around the world, and sit before an audience of strangers passing on the wisdom I'd learned not only through my own experience, but through the experiences of the truly great masters who were my guides and teachers.

We're all buddhas. We just don't recognize it. We are confined in many ways to a limited view of ourselves and the world around us through cultural conditioning, family upbringing, personal experience, and the basic biological predisposition toward making distinctions and measuring present experience and future hopes and fears against a neuronal warehouse of memories.

Once you commit yourself to developing an awareness of your buddha nature, you'll inevitably start to see changes in your day-to-day experience. Things that used to trouble you gradually lose their power to upset you. You'll become intuitively wiser, more relaxed, and more openhearted. You'll begin to recognize obstacles as opportunities for further growth. And as your illusory sense of limitation and vulnerability gradually fades away, you'll discover deep within yourself the true grandeur of who and what you are.

Best of all, as you start to see your own potential, you'll also begin to recognize it in everyone around you. Buddha nature is not a special quality available to a privileged few. The true mark of recognizing your buddha nature is to realize how ordinary it really is—the ability to see that every living creature shares it, though not everyone recognizes it in him- or herself. So instead of closing your heart to people who yell at you or act in some other harmful way, you find yourself becoming more open. You recognize that they aren't "jerks," but are people who, like you, want to be happy and peaceful. They're only acting like jerks because they haven't recognized their true nature and are overwhelmed by sensations of vulnerability and fear.

Your practice can begin with the simple aspiration to do better, to approach all of your activities with a greater sense of awareness and insight, and to open your heart more deeply toward others. Motivation is the single most important factor in determining whether your experience is conditioned by suffering or by peace. Wisdom and compassion actually develop at the same pace. The more attentive you become and the more deeply you examine things, the easier you'll find it to be compassionate. And the more you open your heart to others, the wiser and more attentive you become in all your activities.

At any given moment, you can choose to follow the chain of thoughts, emotions, and sensations that reinforce a perception of yourself as vulnerable and limited—or you can remember that your true nature is pure, unconditioned, and incapable of being harmed. You can remain in the sleep of ignorance or remember that you are and always have been awake. Either way, you're still expressing the unlimited nature of your true being. Ignorance, vulnerability, fear, anger, and desire are expressions of the infinite potential of your buddha nature. There's nothing inherently wrong or right with making such choices. The fruit of Buddhist practice is simply the recognition that these and other mental afflictions are nothing more or less than choices available to us because our real nature is infinite in scope.

We choose ignorance because we *can*. We choose awareness because we *can*. *Samsara* and *nirvana* are simply different points of view based on the choices we make in how to examine and understand our experience. There's nothing magical about *nirvana* and nothing bad or wrong about *samsara*. If you're determined to think of yourself as limited, fearful, vulnerable, or scarred by past experience, know only that you have *chosen* to do so. The opportunity to experience yourself differently is always available.

In essence, the Buddhist path offers a choice between familiarity and practicality. There is, without question, a certain comfort and stability in maintaining familiar patterns of thought and behavior. Stepping outside that zone of comfort and familiarity necessarily involves moving into a realm of unfamiliar experience that may seem really scary—an uncomfortable in-between realm like the one I experienced in retreat. You don't know whether to go back to what was familiar but frightening or to forge ahead toward what may be frightening simply because it's unfamiliar.

In a sense, the uncertainty surrounding the choice to recognize your full potential is similar to what several of my students have told me about ending an abusive relationship: there's a certain reluctance or sense of failure associated with letting go of the relationship.

The primary difference between severing an abusive relationship and entering the path of Buddhist practice is that when you enter the path of Buddhist practice you're ending an abusive relationship with *yourself*. When you choose to recognize your true potential, you gradually begin to find yourself belittling yourself less frequently, your opinion of yourself becomes more positive and wholesome, and your sense of confidence and sheer joy at being alive increases. At the same time, you begin to recognize that everyone around you has the same potential, whether they know it or not. Instead of dealing with them as threats or adversaries, you'll find yourself able to recognize and empathize with their fear and unhappiness. You'll spontaneously respond to them in ways that emphasize solutions rather than problems.

Ultimately, joyful wisdom comes down to choosing between the discomfort of becoming aware of your mental afflictions and the discomfort of being ruled by them. I can't promise you that it will always be pleasant simply to rest in the awareness of your thoughts, feelings, and sensations—and to recognize them as interactive creations of your own mind and body. In fact, I can pretty much guarantee that looking at yourself this way will be, at times, extremely unpleasant.

But the same can be said about beginning anything new, whether it's going to the gym, starting a job, or beginning a diet.

The first few months are always difficult. It's hard to learn all the skills you need to master a job; it's hard to motivate yourself to exercise; and it's hard to eat healthfully every day. But after a while the difficulties subside; you start to feel a sense of pleasure or accomplishment, and your entire sense of self begins to change.

Meditation works the same way. For the first few days you might feel very good, but after a week or so, practice becomes a trial. You can't find the time, sitting is uncomfortable, you can't focus, or you just get tired. You hit a wall, as runners do when they try to add an extra half mile to their exercise. The body says, "I can't," while the mind says, "I should." Neither voice is particularly pleasant; in fact, they're both a bit demanding.

Buddhism is often referred to as the "Middle Way" because it offers a third option. If you just can't focus on a sound or a candle flame for one second longer, then by all means stop. Otherwise, meditation becomes a chore. You'll end up thinking, "Oh, no, it's 7:15. I have to sit down and cultivate awareness." No one ever progresses that way. On the other hand, if you think you could go on for another minute or two, then go on. You may be surprised by what you learn. You might discover a particular thought or feeling behind your resistance that you didn't want to acknowledge. Or you may simply find that you can actually rest your mind longer than you thought you could. That discovery alone can give you greater confidence in yourself.

But the best part of all is that no matter how long you practice, or what method you use, every technique of Buddhist meditation ultimately generates compassion. Whenever you look at your mind, you can't help but recognize your similarity to those around you. When you see your own desire to be happy, you can't avoid seeing the same desire in others. And when you look clearly at your own fear, anger, or aversion, you can't help but see that every-one around you feels the same fear, anger, and aversion.

This is wisdom—not in the sense of book learning, but in the awakening of the heart, the recognition of our connection to oth-ers, and the road to joy.

GLOSSARY

Absolute Bodhicitta The mind that has become completely pure through accomplishing all the levels of training and which, consequently, sees the nature of reality directly, without question or wavering.

Amygdala A small, almond-shaped group of neurons that determine the emotional content of experience.

Application Bodhicitta The path of practice aimed at awakening other people to their full potential. *See also* Bodhicitta, Absolute Bodhicitta, Aspiration Bodhicitta

Aspiration Bodhicitta Cultivating the heartfelt desire to raise all sentient beings to the level at which they completely recognize their true nature. *See also* Bodhicitta, Absolute Bodhicitta, Application Bodhicitta

Attachment Fixed mental and emotional formations about the way things are or should be. *See also* Dzinpa

Aversion The tendency to avoid or eliminate experiences considered unpleasant.

Awareness The capacity to recognize, register, and, in a sense "catalogue" experience. *See also* Pure Awareness, Conditioned Awareness.

Bare Attention A light, gentle awareness of the present moment.

Bindu Sanskrit (Tibetan: tigle): Drops or dots of vital energy propelled through the channels. *See also* Nadi, Prana

Bodhicitta Sanskrit: The "mind of awakening or "awakened mind," a compound term that combines two Sanskrit terms, *bodhi*—which comes from the Sanskrit root verb *budh*, which may be translated as "to become awake, to be come aware, to notice, or to understand" and the word *citta*, which is usually translated as "mind" or sometimes as "spirit" in the sense of "inspiration." *See also* Absolute Bodhicitta, Aspiration Bodhicitta

Buddha Sanskrit: One who is awake to his or her full potential. As a formal title, it usually refers to Gautama Siddhartha.

Buddha Nature The heart or essence of all living beings; an unlimited potential of wisdom, capability, loving-kindness, and compassion.

Capability The power to raise ourselves and others from any condition of suffering.

Clarity A fundamental awareness that allows us to recognize and distinguish among phenomena, it is also a basic characteristic of buddha nature, inseparable from emptiness.

Compassion The aspiration to relieve everyone from the fundamental pain and suffering that stems from not knowing his or her basic nature and the effort we put forth toward achieving relief from that fundamental pain.

Conditioned Awareness A perspective colored by mental and emotional habits arising from ignorance, desire, aversion, and grasping. *See also* Three Poisons, Taṇhā, Trishna, Dzinpa

Desire A craving to acquire or keep whatever we determine as pleasant.

Drenpa Tibetan: To become conscious. *See also* Bare Attention, Mindfulness

Dukkha (pronounced doo-ka) Pali/Sanskrit: A general term for suffering, both extreme and subtle.

Dzinpa Tibetan: Grasping or fixation. *See also* Attachment

Emptiness A rough translation of the Sanskrit *shunyata* and the Tibetan *tongpa-nyi*. An infinitely open space or background that allows for anything to appear, change, disappear, or reappear.

Enlightenment Awakening to the light or potential within us. *See also* Buddha Nature

Four Great Rivers of Suffering Birth, aging, illness, and death.

Four Noble Truths The name applied to the first set of teachings given by the Buddha after he attained enlightenment, which form the basis of all Buddhist traditions. *See also* Three Turnings of the Wheel of Dharma

Gom Tibetan: The common term for meditation; literally, "to become familiar with."

Gross Continuous Impermanence The kinds of changes resulting from causes and conditions that are readily observable. *See also* Impermanence, Subtle Impermanence

Hippocampus A neuronal structure in the brain involved in forming verbal and spatial aspects of memory.

Ignorance Mistaking of distinctions such as "self," "other," "subject," "object," "good," "bad," and other relative distinctions as independently, inherently existing. *See also* Aversion, Desire, and Three Poisons

Impermanence The constant change arising from the ceaseless interplay of multiple causes and conditions. *See also* Gross Continuous Impermanence and Subtle Impermanence

Khorlo Tibtan: The Tibetan equivalent of the Sanskrit term *samsara*. Often interpreted literally as spinning around a wheel.

Kshatriya Sanskrit: The "warrior" class of the Indian caste system.

Lhaktong Tibtan: Literally, "superior seeing" or "seeing beyond." A meditation technique aimed at developing insight into the nature of reality. *See also* Vipashyana

Limbic system A layer of the brain primarily responsible for distinguishing between pain and pleasure, determining emotional responses, and providing a foundation for learning and memory.

Loving-Kindness The desire for everyone to achieve happiness in this life and the effort we put forth to achieve that goal.

Mala Sanskrit: A set of beads used to count repetitions of mantras.

Mantra Sanskrit: Special combinations of ancient syllables that form a sort of prayer or invocation.

Meditative Awareness Approaching thoughts and emotions as objects of focus through which we can achieve a state of mental stability.

Mindfulness The practice of gently welcoming thoughts, emotions, and sensations. *See also* Bare Attention, Drenpa

Nadi Sanskrit (Tibetan: tsa): The channels through which the energy of the body moves. *See also* Prana, Bindu.

Natural Suffering The pain and discomfort we can't avoid in life: birth, aging, illness, and death, as well as natural calamities and unexpected events such as the loss of a friend or loved one. *See also* Four Great Rivers of Suffering and Self-Created Suffering

Neurons Sensory and nervous system cells.

Nirvana Sanskrit: Realization, through direct experience, of our inherently free nature. *See also* Nyang-day

Nyang-day Tibetan: The Tibetan synonym for the Sanskrit term nirvana. Often translated as a state of complete bliss, free from suffering. *See also* Nirvana

Optic Nerve The group of nerve cells that sends messages from a visual system to the visual cortex.

Ordinary Awareness The process of simply noticing phenomena without any express purpose or intention.

Pervasive Suffering The nagging, often unconscious discomfort experienced through moment by moment fluctuations in experience.

Phurba Tibetan: A ritual knife representing the stability of awareness.

Prana Sanskrit (Tibetan: lung): The energy that keeps things moving throughout the body. *See also* Bindhu, Nadi

Puja A religious ritual of devotion

Pure Awareness Awareness unaffected by causes and conditions, or the effects of the Three Poisons. *See also* Clarity, Conditioned Awareness, Boundless Wisdom

Samsara Sanskrit (Tibetan: khorlo): Literally, a wheel. In Buddhist terms, the wheel of suffering; spinning around in the same direction, expecting a different result.

Self-Created Suffering The mental and emotional constructs that we develop in response to natural suffering.

Shamatha Sanskrit: Abiding in calmness; a meditation method for settling the mind. *See also* Shinay

Shinay Tibetan: Literally, abiding in peace or calmness. A meditation technique aimed at allowing the mind to rest. *See also* Shamatha

Stimulus The object of perception.

Stupa Sanskrit: A Buddhist religious monument chiefly representing the enlightened mind of the Buddha, and often including relics of great Buddhist masters.

Subtle Impermanence Changes that occur on a level frequently below that of conscious awareness or perception.

Suffering of Change The discomfort experienced from attachment to pleasurable experience.

Suffering of Suffering The immediate and direct experience of any sort of pain or discomfort.

Sutras Sanskrit: Conversations considered to be actual exchanges between the Buddha and his students.

Taṇhā Pali: Craving, the cause of suffering. *See also* Trishna and Dzinpa

Thalamus A neuronal structure located near the center of the brain, where many of the messages from the senses are sorted before being sent to other areas of the brain.

Three Poisons Habits relating to our experience through ignorance, desire, and aversion that cloud or "poison" awareness.

Three Turnings of the Wheel of Dharma A progressive set of insights into the nature of experience that the Buddha delivered at different stages of his teaching career.

Trishna Sanskrit: Thirst, the Sanskrit term for the cause of suffering.

Vipashyana Sanskrit: Literally, "superior seeing" or "seeing beyond." A meditation technique aimed at developing insight into the nature of reality. *See also* Lhaktong

Visual cortex The area of the brain that translates visual messages received through the optic nerve.

SELECTED BIBLIOGRAPHY

Bennett-Goleman, Tara. *Emotional Alchemy: How the Mind Can Heal the Heart*. New York: Harmony Books, 2001.

Dhammapada, The. Translated by Eknath Easwaran. Tomales, CA: Nilgiri Press, 1985.

Gampopa. *The Jewel Ornament of Liberation*. Translated by Khenpo Konchog Gyaltsen Rinpoche. Edited by Ani K. Trinlay Chödron. Ithaca: Snow Lion Publications, 1998.

Goleman, Daniel. *Emotional Intelligence*. New York: Bantam Books, 1995.

_____. *Destructive Emotions: How Can We Overcome Them?* New York: Bantam Dell, 2003.

Jamgon Kongtrul. *The Torch of Certainty*. Translated by Judith Hanson. Boston and London: Shambhala Publications, Inc., 1977.

Kalu Rinpoche. *The Dharma That Illuminates All Beings Impartially Like the Light of the Sun and the Moon*. Edited by the Kagyu Thubten Choling Translation Committee. Albany: State University Press, 1986.

Khenpo Tsültim Gyamtso. *The Sun of Wisdom: Teachings on the Noble Nagarjuna's Fundamental Wisdom of the Middle Way.* Translated and edited by Ari Goldfield. Boston and London: Shambhala Publications, Inc., 2003.

Patrul Rinpoche. *The Words of My Perfect Teacher,* rev. ed. Translated by the Padmakara Translation Group. Boston: Shambhala Publications, Inc., 1998.

The Ninth Gyalwang Karmapa. *Mahāmudrā: The Ocean of Definitive Meaning.* Translated by Elizabeth M. Callahan. Seattle: Nitartha International, 2001.

The Twelfth Tai Situpa. *Awakening the Sleeping Buddha.* Edited by Lea Terhune. Boston and London: Shambhala Publications, Inc., 1996.

Tulku Urgyen Rinpoche. *As It Is.* Vol 1. Translated by Erik Pema Kunsang. Compiled by Marcia Binder Schmidt. Edited by Kerry Morgan. Hong Kong: Ranjung Yeshe Publications, 1999.

Venerable Dr. Rewata Dhamma. *The First Discourse of the Buddha: Turning the Wheel of Dharma.* Boston: Wisdom Publications, 1997.

ACKNOWLEDGMENTS

EVERY BOOK IS a tapestry of influence and support. In the Buddhist tradition, we depend on those who have received and taken to heart the lessons taught by the Buddha twenty-five hundred years ago. Among the foremost of those who have contributed to my own education—from which this book has evolved—I owe an enormous debt to the teachers who have invested so much time and effort in passing on to me these lessons, including H. E. Tai Situ Rinpoche, H. H. Dilgo Khyentse Rinpoche, Saljay Rinpoche, Nyoshul Khen Rinpoche, my father, Tulku Urgyen Rinpoche, Khenchen Thrangu Rinpoche, Khenchen Kunga Wangchuk Rinpoche, Khenpo Losang Tenzin, Khenpo Tsultrim Namdak, Khenpo Tashi Gyaltsen, Drupon Lama Tsultrim, and my grandfather, Tashi Dorje.

For their unfailing help in providing information and clarification for scientific and psychological issues, I would also like to thank Dr. Richard Davidson and Dr. Antoine Lutz, Daniel Goleman, Tara Bennett-Goleman, and Alex Campbell.

This manuscript would not have come to light without the help of my agent, Emma Sweeney; my publisher, Shaye Areheart; my editor, John Glusman, and his assistant, Anne Berry; marketing manager for Harmony Books, Kira Walton; and all the dedicated people at Harmony Books who, each in his or her own way, have contributed a special brand of insight and wisdom.

I would like to offer very special thanks to Tim and Glenna Olmsted, Josh Baran, Lama Yeshe Gyamtso, Cortland Dahl, and Ani Chudrun, who have offered so much time, effort, and support. I would like to thank my cowriter, Eric Swanson, who worked with great patience in spite of my constant changes to the manuscript. Without him, this book would never have been brought to life.

Most importantly, however, I must thank the people who have attended public teachings and spoken to me in private interviews. They have asked the hardest questions and compelled me to consider the teachings I've received in new and remarkable ways.

INDEX

Abhidharma, 213, 211

abuse, 114, 268
    emotional and verbal, 108, 113, 190, 206
    physical, 108, 190, 206

accidents, 50, 71–72, 155

acupressure, 247

addiction, 11, 45, 53–54, 108, 216

adrenaline, 17, 68, 139

aging, 35, 44–45, 71, 73–76, 77, 106, 107

amygdala, 67–68

Ananda, 123–25

anger, 9, 11, 16, 17, 30, 31, 46, 51, 65, 74, 80, 97, 99, 107, 108, 113, 152, 172, 201, 210, 232–33, 243, 270

anxiety, 10–12, 23–24, 25, 46, 47, 49, 51, 98, 171, 199, 208, 210
    escaping from, 2, 13, 18, 19
    social, 213–14
    succumbing to, 2–3, 32
    working through, 2–3, 4, 28, 31–32

As It Is (Tulku Urgyen Rinpoche), 21

attachment, 129, 175–76, 178, 211
    to beliefs and thoughts, 73–76, 80–82, 100, 101, 102, 104, 106, 160, 178, 225, 236

confrontation of, 115, 169–70, 172
    to things, 70, 72–73

attention, 143–67, 222, 225–40
    to emotions, 30, 86, 97–98, 163–67
    lapses of, 13–15, 18–20, 49, 131, 147, 149, 205
    object-based, 148–51, 152, 159, 177, 190–94, 229
    objectless, 146–48, 156, 162, 163, 166, 177, 180, 188, 190, 196, 230
    practice of, 226–41, 241–42, 244–45, 251–52, 253–54, 258–59
    to sound, 151–54, 158, 159, 180, 229
    to thoughts, 16, 18–20, 26–28, 30, 32, 49, 74, 86, 120, 126–27, 130–31, 148, 159–63, 173, 220–21

"attentional blink," 57, 150–51

aversion, 71, 85, 86, 129, 154, 164, 169, 208, 211, 270

Awakening the Sleeping Buddha (Twelfth Tai Situpa), 94

awareness, 15–20, 84–86, 103, 109, 145–48, 171–74, 210, 226–27, 230, 267
    breathing and, 58–60, 154, 197

ABOUT THE AUTHORS

YONGEY MINGYUR

Yongey Mingyur is one of the most celebrated among the new generation of Tibetan meditation masters. Born in 1975 in Nubri, Nepal, he has been rigorously trained in the practical and philosophical disciplines of Tibetan Buddhism by some of the greatest masters of the Buddhist tradition. Since 1998, he has traveled the world, teaching and counseling thousands of people, and meeting with a diverse array of scientists, including neuroscientists, physicists, and psychologists. His *New York Times* bestselling book *The Joy of Living* has been published in more than a dozen languages. Yongey Mingyur is also the founder of the Tergar Institute in Bodhgaya, India, which is dedicated to providing people with the opportunity to study the classic subjects of the Buddhist tradition and to providing a refuge for deepening their practice of meditation. His candid, often humorous, accounts of his personal difficulties have touched people of all faiths around the world. For more information, please visit www.mingyur.org.

ERIC SWANSON

Coauthor of *The Joy of Living*, Eric Swanson is a graduate of Yale University and the Juilliard School. After formally adopting Buddhism in 1995, Swanson coauthored *Karmapa, The Sacred Prophecy*, a history of the Karma Kagyu Lineage of Tibetan Buddhism. Swanson's second book on Buddhism, *What the Lotus Said,* is a graphic description of his journey to Tibet as a member of a team of volunteers developing schools and medical clinics in rural areas occupied predominantly by nomadic populations.